T0196480

GOD IN US

VISIONS OF OTHER FUTURES

DR. JOHN SJOSTEDT

BALBOA.
PRESS

A DIVISION OF HAY HOUSE

The Authorized (King James) Version of the Bible ('the KJV'), the rights in
which are vested in the Crown in the United Kingdom, is reproduced here
by permission of the Crown's patentee, Cambridge University Press.
The Cambridge KJV text including paragraphing, is reproduced
here by permission of Cambridge University Press.

Balboa Press books may be ordered through booksellers or by contacting:

Balboa Press
A Division of Hay House
1663 Liberty Drive
Bloomington, IN 47403
www.balboapress.com.au
1 (877) 407-4847

Print information available on the last page.

ISBN: 978-1-5043-1343-8 (sc)
ISBN: 978-1-5043-1342-1 (e)

Balboa Press rev. date: 06/28/2018

I dedicate this book to Professor Barbara Thiering of Sydney University, who died on November 16, 2015 and whose research and writings are the inspiration for this story.

CONTENTS

Preface ix

Introduction xi

1   Creation 1

2   The Law of Intended Consequences: Free Will 11

3   Modifying and Moderating Free Will 18

4   The Jews and the Essenes 24

5   Jesus, the Origins of Christianity, and the Bible 34

6   The Divinity of Jesus and the Christian Church 41

7   Parallels between Christianity and Paganism 59

8   God in Us 67

9   God in Us: Attaining Enlightenment 79

10 God in Us: The Presence of Evil 86

11 God in Us: When God Becomes Wanton 94

12 God in Us: Lucifer's Tale 102

13 Addendum: An Analysis of Understanding Elohim 129

Conclusion 143

Epilogue 145

PREFACE

I started my autobiography on December 26, 2016, and finished it on March 31, 2017, apart from a growing number of addenda and sidebars, as I call them. This was an interesting experience for me, as I have wanted to write for almost all my life but could never seem to find something to get started on.

Being a huge fan of J.K. Rowling and Stephanie Meyer, I started writing a book of fantasy, with witches, wizards, and the like. I got to about three-quarters of the way into writing the book (maybe 150 to 160 pages), but I couldn't see the conclusion. What I could see didn't seem to have the suspense or zing I wanted. So, I temporarily hung-up my book of fantasy entitled *Gabriel and Thor the Dog of War: World War I*. I then started my autobiography to keep myself writing.

Now, I've start this current book, *God in Us: Visions of Other Futures,* and my Gabriel book continues to languish, though I now have some ideas with which to continue. I've changed the title of *God in Us* half a dozen times so far. It will be controversial if it ever becomes known or, heaven forbid, published.

INTRODUCTION

I was sitting up in bed, meditating, as I do, rugged up against the cold in my jacket, with my maroon meditation shawl draped around my shoulders. My beautiful cattle dog–cross, Heidi, was pretending to be asleep on the bed, waiting for me to get up and throw balls for her or take her for her daily drive in Pugsley, my Peugeot 207, as these were things we typically did on my days off work. My darling kelpie-cross, Bonnie, was flat out on the floor, snoring—no pretence there. My dogs belong to a special breed, fondly called "layabout," and my two girls are exponents of the art. The ship's cat is called Sailor. She is a feline version of layabout, though distantly related.

I usually mediate for an hour to an hour and a half, but because I am warm and comfortable, sometimes my meditation may be interrupted by my slipping into the low theta λ (7-4 cycles per second [cps]) or delta Δ (4 cps) brain rhythm, which equates to sleep.

So, it was Thursday morning, May 25, 2017, at about 6:00 a.m., I was meditating, and an idea sprang into my mind. I was not thinking about anything; my form of mediation is an adaption of Vipassana meditation, where I clear my mind of all thoughts and allow ideas to materialise, if they are to materialise.

My meditation is encapsulated in the following Japanese Haiku (俳句):

Sitting quietly, doing nothing, spring comes,
the grass grows by itself.

My mind was clear, and I was not meditating on any theme. As I meditated, an idea formed in my mind. I do not know if I was asleep or awake. In mindless meditation, time passes instantaneously; there is no awareness of time passing.

In my autobiography (the first draft of which had just been completed), in the closing chapters, I had been exploring religion and my experiences within the Christian religion. I had also been reading and studying the work of Professor Barbara Thiering, researcher into the Dead Sea Scrolls and author of *The Qumran Origins of the Christian Church*[1]. Professor Thiering's book is a very difficult and dense read. Obviously, it was written for researchers in the field and not for a layman like me. Still, I had been dwelling on the complexities of Professor Thiering's work. It was on my mind.

During that early morning, I received a message. I felt it was from God Himself, or maybe my guardian-angel *Elohim*. (I have christened her Lisa, though she might be a bloke— that would be very disappointing. More about the Elohim as this story unfolds.) Now, if you read my autobiography and even my book of fantasy, I am rather scathing in my condemnation of those individuals who "hear" the voice of God, or archangels and the like, either in their heads or for real. I even unkindly labelled Moses as an undiagnosed

---

[1] E. Thiering, *The Qumran Origins of the Christian Church:*(Sydney: Theological Explorations, 1983).

schizophrenic. My contention is that if *you* yourself have never heard a voice from heaven on high (and neither have I), then those who do hear voices are hallucinating.

Nevertheless, this message or idea formed in my mind. It seemed to coalesce some of the ideas about God and our perceived relationship with God that I had been considering and mulling over for months, even years. This book is about that coalescence of ideas.

My first idea was that God is an unprovable hypothesis. I cannot prove that God exists, and you cannot prove that He doesn't.

I am what is commonly called an agnostic. In this earthly realm, I consider that God is unknown and unknowable. Nevertheless, I look around me, and I see the perfection of our world—where greedy humans have not ruined it—and I find it hard not to see God in it. My acknowledgement of my stance as an agnostic is now somewhat at odds with my latest glimpse of my "visions of other futures," as I call them.

So, I first sought to attempt to fathom some of the depths of God and what He has created. A very tall task indeed for a self-confessed agnostic. He created one of seven universes, together with his six companions, all of whom created their own universes. He also created living spiritual beings, the first of whom He named Michael then Lucifer—the Morning Star, or the Shining One—soon to be followed by many other such beings. They became the Lord God's helpers; they were His companions and His family.

In the Hebrew language, God is called *Yahweh Elohim*, or the Lord God. In creating Michael and Lucifer, He commenced the creation of a group of beings the Hebrew tongue collectively named *Elohim*, a uniplural word (like the

English word *sheep*) for God, gods, and objects of worship. Those Elohim helped Yahweh Elohim harness the power of the *singularity* that followed, which our scientists call the Big Bang; the Elohim also helped to create galaxies, suns, solar systems, and planets.[2]

In trying to fathom Yahweh Elohim, it follows that one is confronted with tales of the Elohim. Prominent among those tales are stories—myths, really—about the Arch-Elohim Lucifer and other arch-Elohim, such as Michael and Gabriel. An Elohim called Jesus and his group of friends is also prominent, working together to subdue Planet Earth from its chaotic state following the singularity. The Elohim Jesus helped play a major role in the first appearance of human beings (*Homo sapiens*) on Planet Earth, some 200,000 years ago. These humans were created in the image of the Elohim, by the Elohim themselves.

The story of the creation of human beings on Planet Earth is intertwined with the story of the Jewish people, their twelve tribes, and their adventures in Egypt, wandering for forty years in the Sinai Desert and eventually settling in Palestine. We hear stories about not only the broader Jewish nation but also sects within the Jewish religion: the Essenes, the Zealots, the Pharisees, and the Sadducees. Interestingly, the Elohim Jesus appears again, this time as a human being and an important member of the Essene sect of Judaism. Jesus was acknowledged as the kingly Jewish Messiah, with his familial lineage in the line of the Jewish King David.

---

[2] This universe is estimated to be 13.772 BY (billion years) old. Our galaxy, the Milky Way, is estimated to be about 13.21 BY old, and Planet Earth is 4.543 BY old. Our solar system and Planet Earth are on the outer edge of one of the spiral arms of our galaxy.

The appearance of the Elohim Jesus as a human being living among the Essenes, raised many questions in me. Why was Jesus, an Elohim, one of the gods, on Planet Earth among the Essenes? How and why was he human—if, indeed, he *was* human—and were the stories about his miraculous birth, as well as the many miracles he was reputed to have performed, true?

That Jesus was regarded as a god by the humans he and his companions created on earth is understandable. But, was he wholly human, as the man Jesus at the Essene settlement of Qumran situated near the Dead Sea, or was he a god, an Elohim still, posing as a man? It is understood that Elohim, being spirit, do not need to eat or sleep; they cannot die or feel pain in any physical sense. So, did Jesus really endure the pain of physical torture, humiliation, crucifixion, and near death on the cross, as a human man? Did Jesus rise from the dead, miraculously healed by the Lord God through the agency of Simon Magus? Did Jesus ascend into heaven, where he became part of the Holy Trinity with the Lord God and the Holy Spirit?

These were intriguing questions confronting me. There appears to be much mythology about the Elohim and, particularly, Jesus. Sorting out fact from myth and the reality of what was the true gospel of Jesus, his Good News, was not straightforward. It seemed clear that Jesus would not be accused of blasphemy and would not have been nailed to a cross if he had merely claimed he was a son or child of God. The idea that we are all children of the Lord God was well accepted among the Jews and the Essenes, and even some other religions of the world. But to have been accused of blasphemy, as he was, Jesus's gospel would, of necessity, have been much more confrontational, powerful, and potent than what is commonly broadcast by the religions then and today.

Unravelling the content of Jesus's true gospel became a very interesting adventure, the story of which is revealed in the following pages of this book. Jesus said: "... Ye are Gods," which was blasphemy to the Jews, particularly the Essenes. In effect, he said: "You, all of you, are gods, and I am god too." To his opponents, that statement was blasphemy, and that is why they tortured and crucified him.

———◇◇◇———

Finally, in addition to Professor Barbara Thiering's works, I have been studying some of the works of Dr Doreen Virtue. Dr Virtue has been a clairvoyant from childhood and teaches the metaphysical courses that she describes in her books. I find her work informative and fascinating, and I wondered how her work *Earth Angels*[3] relates to the topic of this book.

She makes the point that there is only one source of power in this universe, only one Creator. She said it better and more succinctly than I have here, but the essence is that we, she and I, agree: there is only one God and one Creator, whether she calls Him God, or I call Him Yahweh Elohim (or the Lord God). What Dr Virtue calls "Earth Angels," I call "Elohim" (gods, objects of worship, according to my concordance of the Bible).

Whilst Dr Virtue divides "Earth Angels" into five subdivisions ("Incarnated Angels," "Incarnated Elements,"

---

[3] D. Virtue, *Earth Angels* (Carlsbad, United States: Hay House, Inc., 2002).

"Star People," "Walk-Ins," and "The Wise Ones"), I have only three categories. What she calls "Archangels" and "Guardian Angels," I call arch-Elohim and guardian Elohim. What she calls "Incarnated Angels," I call Elohim (or gods). Dr Virtue describes us all as "Angels," including the Elohim Jesus, or the human being Jesus on earth two thousand years ago.

The Elohim, however, are not truly God/gods, in the same sense that our God, our Creator, is the one and only power in our universe. The Elohim is the term that the simple human beings the Elohim created in their image called them, according to the book of Genesis in the Bible. The Elohim, however, gave all recognition for the creation of human beings to the Lord God; as do Dr Virtue and me.

Dr Virtue clearly states that some "Earth Angels" came from other planets and other solar systems, perhaps even from other galaxies. I have not made that leap in this book, though I imagine that it is entirely possible and even likely. I have centred my story around Planet Earth and the events that sources like the Bible discuss.

<hr>

Jeremy, a highly intelligent friend, to whom I gave the book to read and comment upon, suggested the book needed a central character. I had not considered this, and I wondered how I might incorporate his idea into this book. So, I put the idea out into the universe and the hands of God and the Elohim and came up with the idea of have three main characters, if not central characters, which would form a small panel of arch-Elohim commentators. The first one would be Lucifer, then Gabriel and Michael, and, perhaps, even Jesus, a fourth commentator, at times. (As I write this, I have no idea how this will work out. So, I'm saving this version of the book, in its present evolution and starting a new version. I'll let you know if the new version works out.)

<hr>

I am a psychological research scientist, psychologist, counsellor, hypnotherapist and psychotherapist. I am not an astrophysicist or galactic astronomer. So, the story I am about to relate is outside of my immediate field. I say "story" because I don't know if it's real, a true reality, or if it is a delusion of my mind. Many would say I'm delusional.

CHAPTER 1

CREATION

The word *creation* presumes a creator. In terms of the universe, without a Creator, all happened by random chance. Without a Creator, the complexity of an eye and the perfection of a leaf are all proposed to have happened by random chance over aeons.

The power of the Spirit, or Essence, could not be quantified. Where the Spirit came from was unknown and unknowable. It existed, and it was beyond any understanding of the word *intelligent.*

At some point, the Spirit divided into seven distinct entities: each with free will, and each in the image of the others. These entities began their work. Events that aeons later started the creation process from absolutely nothing— nothing at all—would be called the *Big Bang.*

Matter is comprised of elemental gases (codified as, for example, O, N, Ni, He, Ne, and H) and elemental chemicals (codified as, for example, Na, Mg, Ca, K, and Zn) that would eventually constitute the Periodic Table of the Elements, which scientists assembled to classify the known elements of our universe. This matter—these gases and minerals—began to expand. Again, aeons later, the central core of this cosmic event—the so-called Big Bang, the creation of matter where none had existed before—would be called a *singularity*. The Spirit, seeing this singularity, named Himself, Herself, or Itself—Himself seems more appropriate—the *One*. Whilst there was no physical form to smile, the ghost of a smile would certainly have formed on His lips.

Thus, the One had no physical form, unlike the matter He created. He set about experimenting with some forms of physical appearance. Strangely, the six other nonphysical selves might be considered His *friends*, or His *brothers* and *sisters*, now that they had come to the same conclusion that a physical form must be considered if His (and their) work was to be successfully understood and accomplished. As with all brothers and sisters, there was a growing sense of gender differences, even though they were born of the same source.

"What was that work?" you might ask the One or any of these six others, whom I refer to collectively, throughout, as the Ones.

The Ones would reply, "The creation of Our universe."

We might get the impression that this work was being directed by some greater force, or Spirit, that was even more unknown and unknowable.

There was no pattern or template in existence here. There were no previously existing physical laws. All physical laws were newly created and newly devised by the lawgivers (the Ones, and each, perhaps, was slightly different from the others). As the unimaginable density and heat generated by the singularity expanded, the clouds of gases and minerals cooled from the unimaginably intense heat and pressure of the singularity, forming into the superheated, swirling arms of galaxies. This includes billions of galaxies spinning through space, guided by the Ones' newly created immutable laws. Though the Ones are omniscient and omnipotent, sometimes errors were made. Planets sometimes collided; thus, Planet Earth's moon was formed.

As the galaxies spun, suns were formed and spun off, and billions and billions of suns and solar systems were formed from superheated gases and minerals. These, in turn, created planets and gaseous nebulae of ionised space dust and gases, such as helium and hydrogen. This process was the creation of our Milky Way galaxy and of our lives—as gods and humans.

The seven universes (of the seven Ones) began to take shape. However, each shape was slightly different, as the free will and personality of each of the Ones slowly formed, separately and distinctly. To clarify, they were not entirely separate from each other, as their minds were interconnected. An idea formed in the mind of One was instantly available to all the Ones. For instance, our One—as we could later call Him—started developing the idea of helpers and companions. Aeons later, in the Hebrew language of the tribes of Judah, these beings would be called *Elohim* (gods, objects of worship, or the Lord God of our universe).

Time could exist now. With only the Ones' nebulous and, perhaps, initially unformed ideas of creating their universes and, ultimately, habitable galaxies, solar systems, and planets, time could not exist. Time could only exist where a concept of distance existed, and distance on a universal scale could only be imagined or visualised by those who possessed mortality. The immortals, the Elohim and Yahweh Elohim, those with everlasting life, could only have the barest concept of time. Yet a physical universe, governed by physical laws created by the immortal ones, would be bound and always constrained by distance and, thus, time.

The Ones began to understand and appreciate these new concepts more fully and more clearly as their physical universes began to coalesce into galaxies, solar systems, and potentially habitable planets.

At some point, billions of years ago, our One created beings who were essentially spirit but could materialise and take physical form. Our One called the first two of them: Michael – who is like God and Lucifer—the Morning Star, or the Shining One—and they were endowed with free will. Our One was pleased with Michael and Lucifer, Elohim, and so He created numerous other Elohim. Lucifer, the second being created by our One, was perhaps seen as one of the most senior beings, but still an Elohim, as were his Elohim brothers and Elohim sisters. Hundreds of thousands of Elohim were created and individually named by our One, Yahweh Elohim, and He set them to assist in the creation of His (and our) universe.

Each of the Ones had a common origin, but because of free will, individual differences developed. So, too, did the phenomenon of free will develop in each Elohim. They each took on their own individuality and appearance, just as happened with humans, much later—billions of years later, in fact. All human beings, because of free will, have their own individual personalities and appearances.

Our One was pleased with His creation and saw that some individual Elohim seemed more talented and industrious than others. He presumed it might be the same in most families, for he saw His Elohim as His family and not merely His creation. He noticed Michael, Raphael, Gabriel, Uriel, Saraqael, Raguel, and Remiel, as well as Lucifer, and called them *arch-Elohim*, but they would later be known as *archangels* or *guardian angels*. Our One also noticed one of His later creations—an intelligent and enthusiastic Elohim—and bestowed upon him and his friends the honour of leading our One's special creation: Project Planet Earth. This was the creation of Planet Earth from the chaos and confusion following the singularity that resulted in the coalescence of gas, dust, and minerals into our physical galaxies, solar systems, and planets.

This group of friends was assembled under the guiding hand of Lucifer, who was responsible for the entire Milky Way Galaxy Project and numerous other galaxies. They called themselves the Project Planet Earth Task Force. They were led by the Elohim nicknamed AC, or Alpha Centauri, the name of a star system he loved. AC was the talented and industrious Elohim noticed by our One and was the driving force behind Project Planet Earth. He and his friends were each identified by the initials PPE (Project Planet Earth), followed by an identifier or nickname of their own choice. These included BE, for Bright Eyes; BM, for Big Momma; and HL, for Hot Lips (to mention but a few of these nicknames). They worked tirelessly under the direct auspices of the Archangel Lucifer, who was extraordinarily busy. With AC, work was both challenging and fun.

Our Planet Earth, it is said, came into being 4.543 billion years (BY) ago as a molten glob of superheated gases, elemental materials, and space dust. Eventually, Earth cooled and was completely covered by raging seas and oceans. Many aeons later, the PPEs set to work creating land masses where only oceans had existed. This was a first for the Elohim AC and his team of one hundred friends. Together, they had seen the formation of galaxies, suns, solar systems, and planetary systems. They had helped guide the formation of those bodies, but they had performed no intricate work themselves.

The first job of Project Planet Earth was to pacify the raging sea and somehow absorb the dense, thick rain cloud that shrouded Planet Earth, thereby allowing the sun to shine through the clouds. They were then able to make Planet Earth fit for vegetative life, for animal and bird life, and, eventually, for humankind: men and women who looked like Yahweh Elohim and the other Elohim of His creation who would eventually populate all seven of the universes. The populating of Planet Earth with men and women in the image of the Elohim was our One's ultimate dream, which He hadn't shared with any other being.

In many places on earth, volcanoes existed, thrusting above the oceans and the earth's crust. The crust was unstable and drowned in the earth's encircling waters. So, whilst it was not dangerous work for immortal spirit beings like Elohim to undertake this project, it was tricky, painstaking work to ensure that the land masses, once formed, were not inundated and reconsumed by the raging oceans and howling winds.

Over aeons, land masses were deliberately formed and raised higher, and polar ice caps were formed. They stored much of the excess seawater great distances beneath the surface of the oceans, in their abysmal depths.

With the seas somewhat more manageable, if not completely subdued, AC and his friends set themselves to facilitating light to shine upon earth through the heavy, thick, atmospheric, rain-bearing clouds that completely shrouded the planet, cutting off all light and plunging the earth's surface into almost perpetual darkness. Calming of the raging sea helped with this task, and, eventually, our sun shone patchily upon earth and the oceans, through the cloud cover.

With light from our sun shining upon earth, plants, including grasses and trees, had light to grow. Over time, not only land vegetation but also seagrasses, algae, and kelp began to flourish, enriching the oceans. These plants were supplied by the universe of another of the Ones—Universe Three, which specialised in plants: trees, grasses, grains, and the like.

Later writers will say that the creation of land masses, and the calming of the seas and other creation events that followed, each took only one day: the first day, second day, and the like. This is arrant nonsense. It took hundreds of thousands of years for the seas and the climate to come under the control of AC and his friends. So those "days" must be viewed as mere conceptual dividers, not physical twenty-four-hour Planet Earth days.

Billions of years earlier, perhaps around 4.00 BY ago—possibly even before our One created Michael and Lucifer and any other of the Elohim—while earth was still hot and molten, it is believed that the moon was created as the result of a large planetary body, perhaps the size of Mars, colliding with earth. Today, some scientists call it the Big Splash or the Giant Impact hypothesis. However, once the oceans were quelled and the atmospheric clouds slowly dissipated, the sun, the moon, and the stars in the night sky became visible from earth. Supposedly, this was the fourth day.

About 230 million years ago, AC's fellow Elohim then set about planning for the creation of living creatures on the land and in the seas and the oceans. Because of the surprising quickness of their taming of Planet Earth's atmosphere, AC was called to visit our One, who was surprised and delighted by the progress. He took AC on a grand tour of the universe to view the progress being made. Our One and AC toured for a mere two to three hundred years.

In the meantime, AC's friends and workers on Project Planet Earth, under the periodic guidance of Lucifer, started to create creatures like dinosaurs—tyrannosaurus, triceratops, stegosaurus, and maybe even the forebears of rhinoceros and crocodiles. They created land-based velociraptors and pterodactyls that could be seen flying in the cloudy skies. They were beautiful creatures, in the most powerful of senses, and might have been wonderfully adapted for a more rugged existence on many other planets. But they were not suited to Planet Earth. The unfortunate problem with these creations of the enthusiastic and well-meaning workers of Project Planet Earth was that, in our One's mind, the culmination of the work of AC and the PPE team would be the creation of human beings in the image of the Elohim that He Himself created. Our One and AC had discussed the plans and intentions for Project Planet Earth as they toured the universe together, and AC knew that it was our One's intention to populate the earth with human beings, as they called them. However, the animals that his friends and co-workers had created on the land, in the oceans, and in the skies, were all completely unsuited to accompany human life on Planet Earth. The creation of human life was our One's central interest, and humans could not survive a rampaging Tyrannosaurus rex.

It is fortunate, with foresight and intent, that each

universe specialised in different living creatures. As already mentioned, one universe specialised in plants—trees, grasses, and flowers of every kind; another specialised in the formation of different land and soil types, along with the living organisms that populated the soil; another specialised in sea creatures; another specialised in birds; and yet another specialised in land-based animals that would be entirely compatible with our universe's specialisation in human beings created in the image of the Elohim—both males and females.

So, various kinds of animal types were moved from one universe (Universe Two) to our universe (Universe One) by *desculators* (later called "wormholes"). Upon entering a desculator, the humans or animals would immediately—instantaneously, in fact—emerge at their respective destinations. And so, animals that were much friendlier and more adaptable, though still wild and dangerous to humankind, were placed in a deep sleep and painlessly transported to earth, which was now ready for them. The transportation of sea creatures from the Universe Four, which specialised in the creation of friendlier and more-adaptive sea creatures, also provided fish, whales, sharks, crustaceans of every kind, and even crocodiles for our universe.

Next, around 400,000 years ago, after a series of false starts and trials with males and females resembling semi-upright and upright hairy apes—*Pithecanthropus erectus,* Java man, and *Homo erectus,* and, perhaps, even the Neanderthal subspecies of *Homo sapiens*—our universe finally emerged, about 200,000 years ago, with men and women in the image of the Elohim—*Homo sapiens,* or modern man, as present-day scientists eventually called the species which emerged. This, of course, allowed our universe to supply male and female human beings to populate the other six universes.

What of the less-adaptable species of animals (the animal/dinosaur false start) made by AC's friends during his absence whilst on the grand tour of the universe with our One)? A cataclysmic event resulting in atmospheric change on a planetary scale, perhaps caused by another collision with a large planetary body, wiped out the dinosaurs. Though this was a planetary-wide disaster, it was in some ways fortunate, because Elohim are not permitted to purposely cause death or destruction to any living creature. In fact, doing so will result in the forfeiture and revocation of their own eternal life. The death of all the dinosaurs was outside the control of AC and his friends; they were not responsible.

After earth recovered from the cataclysmic atmospheric event that killed the dinosaurs, AC and his crew were kept very busy supervising the teleportation via desculators of human beings, each in a deep sleep, to each of the other universes. Once the pattern for the creation of males and females in the image of the Elohim was firmly established, it became an easy matter to create a human population on earth and elsewhere.

AC and his friends, humble beings that they were, could justly feel proud of their efforts. This was the start of the human population of all seven universes, but Planet Earth was the first.

CHAPTER 2

THE LAW OF INTENDED CONSEQUENCES: FREE WILL

We may all have heard of the *law of unintended consequences:* things that the gods and humankind do that result in consequences beyond their intent, scope, and control. The law of intended consequences occurs when omniscient beings allow the thoughts and behaviours of humankind (women and men) and the gods (Elohim) to develop and unfold without the intervention of the Ones, the omnipotent and omniscient beings of the seven universes. This allows humankind and the gods the freedom and free will to develop outside the control of Yahweh Elohim. This action could be called *noninterventionism,* and that, to a point, is correct. It allows all beings, both humans and gods, the capacity to exercise their free will and to live with the consequences of their free will. Otherwise, how would they learn?

Yahweh Elohim, the Lord God of our universe (Universe One), is loving, kind, considerate, and generous. His generosity extended to His intention to give Planet Earth to the Elohim

AC and his companions, as a reward for their steadfastness, single-mindedness, and tenacity in seeing the creation and re-creation of Project Planet Earth into its state as the first human-populated planet in any universe, anywhere. This was a mammoth and praiseworthy achievement, but there was no sense of egotistical pride in AC or his companions, who were all quite equally responsible for the re-creation and population of Planet Earth.

Free will, personal responsibility and accountability comprise Yahweh Elohim's, and all the other Ones', agreed-upon and chosen philosophy and mode of living in all seven universes. However, it was jointly understood and appreciated by all seven Ones that free will could potentially allow the development of character flaws in some susceptible Elohim.

Free will allows beings to have full and unfettered expression of themselves, their potentialities, and their personalities. But free will could also allow the development of flagrant egoism and egotism, perhaps a sense of undeserved self-centredness, and even narcissism, that would prevent them from showing love concern and compassion for their fellow spirit beings, for created human beings, and for animals.

Free will could allow the development of barely controlled anger that might lead to violence or destruction, and even forbidden death and killing, by some Elohim. In others, pride might develop; in still others, a sense of gratuitous entitlement might develop, along with other flaws of the ego.

AC and his companions were simple, humble Elohim who neither expected nor wanted a reward for their efforts. Their labour of love was in the transformation of earth from the confused and chaotic state it had been in, to the habitable planet they made it, which included populating earth with living creatures from other universes and, of course, the creation of humankind (males and females).

Naturally, the Elohim who created the Planet Earth's human beings were seen and recognised as gods by the simple, unsophisticated men and women whom the Elohim had created in their own images. But, though they were treated as gods, they always gave the glory and recognition to Yahweh Elohim—for everything.

The ceremony and recognition of the Elohim AC by Yahweh Elohim, and the proposed gift of Planet Earth to AC and his companions, raised a sense of resentment in Lucifer. Whilst he had not worked on Planet Earth to any great extent, he was one of the great ones: an archangel among his fellow Elohim. He felt hurt that Yahweh Elohim had not given him some form of the recognition accorded to AC. Consequently, Lucifer spoke out to Yahweh Elohim concerning his feelings.

Yahweh Elohim recognised Lucifer's feelings for what they truly were: false pride driven by ego, one of the perceived and predicted personality flaws of free will. He, Yahweh Elohim, freely chose to change His decision, and gave dominion over the Planet Earth to Lucifer and his trusted companions for one thousand years. AC and his companions freely accepted Yahweh Elohim's decision, without complaint or resentment.

In the Bible, it is recorded that, to Yahweh Elohim, "a day is as a thousand years and a thousand years is as a day." So, the period that Lucifer would have dominion over Planet Earth is an indeterminant period. A day has past, as has a thousand years, so that leaves "a thousand years as a day," which could be interpreted as 365,000 years. This is a little problematic, as the species of humans ultimately created by AC and his group, culminating in *Homo sapiens* (modern males and females), supposedly came into existence about 200,000 years ago. Still, the only point-of-time option that we have left is the 365,000-year option. This might mean that Lucifer will continue to preside over Planet Earth for an additional 165,000 years (that is, 365,000 minus 200,000 equals 165,000 years), or thereabout, unless Yahweh Elohim chooses another course of action and, perhaps, cuts the time short, with the agreement of Lucifer.

When reading in the Bible and other sources the account of our Yahweh Elohim changing His mind and giving Planet Earth to Lucifer and his band of loyal followers, we find Lucifer descending to take over dominion of Planet Earth. Sometime later, he was followed to Planet Earth by one-third of the "heavenly host."

It is written that this sizable group of Elohim came to earth, separate from Lucifer and his band, to have sexual intercourse with the Planet Earth's males and females that had been created by AC and his friends. However, when they tried to return to the heavenly realm, where Yahweh Elohim and the other two-thirds of the heavenly host remained, they found their return blocked by the Archangel Michael. Presumably, this means that they, the host, had to remain on earth at Yahweh Elohim's pleasure—perhaps until Lucifer's reign on earth is over and he returns to Yahweh Elohim's heavenly realm. (Some scenarios addressing the possibilities in store for the one-third of the heavenly host will be discussed later.)

How many is "one-third of the heavenly host"? We

don't really know. However, the New Testament's book of Revelation talks about when AC and his group of Elohim's return to Planet Earth to take possession of the gift given to them by Yahweh Elohim: some 144,000 elect rule the universe, together with Yahweh Elohim in His heavenly realm. So, if my math is up to it—and there is no guarantee that it is—and the 144,000 is the group of Elohim who remained with Yahweh Elohim in His heavenly realm and did not visit earth's humans, that would comprise the two-thirds. Then, if 144,000 Elohim equals two-thirds of the heavenly host, the one-third of the heavenly host who came to earth would equal 96,000 Elohim. This means that Yahweh Elohim initially created 240,000 (144,000 plus 96,000), or nearly a quarter of a million Elohim, to help Him create our universe. The number of Elohim workers seems a little light for the job. (Of course, this is all interesting speculation. The Bible and other written sources are mostly silent on these matters. Nevertheless, some very interesting questions and issues arise for our consideration. We will address these issues in a series of scenarios later.)

Meanwhile, what did the faithful Elohim AC and his band, and the remainder of the heavenly host, do in heaven when the others were on Planet Earth having their nefarious way with the earthlings? Did they, the faithful Elohim, remain in heaven and gaze at the "beatific vision" for all future eternity? That would be boring, I think. (Of course, it makes for a great Catholic doctrine; sort of in the league of the doctrines of heaven, hell, purgatory, and limbo [or *limbus infantium* or *limbus puerorum*].)[4]

No, I do not consider that they gazed at the so-called beatific vision. I reckon that the faithful Elohim remained in heaven with Yahweh Elohim, and they may have had sexual or loving relationships with each other. After all, they created man and women in their own image, and humans can have sex. Therefore, I suppose, so, too, can the Elohim, and even Yahweh Elohim, if He, She, or It so desires—that would be a supercharged blast, wouldn't it, if you were the lucky girl or boy!

(We are delving into the deepest of speculation here, but I don't think He minds. This is a story, after all.)

What else did the faithful Elohim do? We know that AC and his friends re-created Planet Earth and populated it with males and females: Caucasians, Egyptians, Arabs, Chinese, Slavs, Africans, Mexicans, and all other distinct human races. It is interesting to consider that Yahweh Elohim obviously wanted and prized variation and diversity in the creation He ordained. The other faithful Elohim, in all likelihood, continued the creation process, directed by the arch-Elohim and under the supervision of Yahweh Elohim. They may also have created or populated other human colonies on favourable planets in other suitable solar systems—remember that there are potentially billions of galaxies in our universe alone, with innumerable solar systems in each galaxy.

---

[4] Wikipedia; Wikipedia's entry for *Limbus Infantium* or *Limbus Puerorum*.

If free will, personal responsibility, and accountability represent the central philosophy of Yahweh Elohim in all seven universes, and if serious character flaws can arise with the application of free will, how can these character flaws be addressed and eradicated?

CHAPTER 3

MODIFYING AND
MODERATING FREE WILL

As we have seen with AC and his crew, not every Elohim is filled with rampant pride and arrogant egotism; neither is every human being so negatively endowed. In fact, whilst it was widely held and accepted by Yahweh Elohim and the six others that the application of free will is potentially susceptible to misuse and abuse by Elohim and human beings alike, not all Elohim or humans are susceptible to the gross personality and character flaws that could result from the misuse of free will.

The proper use of free will can, and does, lead to love, compassion, consideration, and respect. However, improper use of free will can, and does, lead to egotism, narcissism, disrespect, lack of love and concern for others, and even destruction and death. It is the positive results of the application of free will that guides, leads, and excites Yahweh Elohim and the six others.

Nevertheless, it is held by many that the spirit of the Elohim is fixed and immutable and very difficult, if not impossible, to modify or moderate by any "normal" means.

If this is correct, we seem to have arrived at an impasse. But, naturally, Yahweh Elohim and all six of the others, in their omniscience, had considered this matter and foreseen this impasse.

Naturally, they found a solution: the application of the *human experience*, the *human life force*, the state of *being a human*—whichever term you prefer—a state of being that is almost infinitely modifiable and adjustable. Surprisingly, being human can modify spirit. In other words, becoming human, living as a human being, can moderate the spirit of Elohim—even the Spirit of Yahweh Elohim, if it came to that. But, obviously to a being, an Elohim, enjoying immortality and everlasting life, who has helped create a universe under the auspices of that universe's Yahweh Elohim and who now has dominion over that universe, the idea of humbling the self and becoming human would be a very daunting and even unwelcome experience. (This is particularly true in regard to that bit about dying, as described in the *Elohim User's Handbook*. Obviously, many Elohim would want to give that experience a wide berth, or even a complete miss, if humanly or even inhumanly possible.)

Under free will, of course, each being—Elohim and human alike—has the freedom to experience the human life force and human nature in order to achieve and develop the desired positive attributes of free will: love, compassion, consideration, and respect. Yet, we look around us and can see the improper application of free will in many human beings and even, perhaps, among Elohim.

Elohim may have been among us for millennia, and we would have never known. Elohim living on this Planet Earth who have not yet been allowed to return to Yahweh Elohim's heavenly realm have been living among us for hundreds of thousands of years. They are ageless and indestructible, but ordinary human beings would never know of their existence, having already died during the course of the existence of the Elohim. The Elohim who came to earth after Lucifer—perhaps a little less than 200,000 years ago—may have never changed. However, the wise Elohim would have learned and grown from their experience upon earth, exactly as desired and intended by our Yahweh Elohim regarding their sojourn here.

In the previous chapter, we explored some interesting issues and questions arising from the possible presence of Elohim among us. It is estimated that there may have been a heavenly host of some 240,000 Elohim initially created by our One. Some 96,000 (or one-third) of the heavenly host is reported to have come to Planet Earth to have their way with the humans soon after Lucifer came to earth to take up the thousand-year reign that our Yahweh Elohim assigned to him.

So, let us consider two scenarios that might have played out with one-third of the heavenly host on Planet Earth.

Scenario 1: Yahweh Elohim's restriction on their return to the heavenly realm was very short-lived. Let us call this group *Randy 96K*. They were required by Yahweh Elohim's Archangel Michael to remain on Planet Earth to consider the errors of their ways and were eventually allowed to return to Yahweh Elohim's heavenly realm after a very brief time, a matter of a few earth weeks, months, or, perhaps, years.

However, we might consider the effect that the Randy 96K

had upon the earth's human population, which was probably quite small, compared with today's population—maybe just two million souls. This argument is jumping the gun, so to speak, but assuming the Elohim are sexually fertile—and we can know this by the veracity of certain events that will be discussed later—then there might have been a small population boom on earth, and in the heavenly realm as well. This would include pregnancies of female Elohim by human males, if there were no means of supernatural contraception and, likewise, pregnancies of human women by male Elohim.

There are many variables in this situation that are not known. Again, we are delving into the area of speculation.

Scenario 2: The Randy 96K have remained on Planet Earth for a little less than 200,000 years, or about 6,667 thirty-year generations, the length of time that scientists consider *Homo sapiens,* as a species, has been on earth. Whilst mathematicians would find this puzzle beyond easy to calculate, there are too many unknown variables for us to give an estimate of how many present-day humans have the blood of the Elohim running through their veins. However, the compounding effects of population growth would possibly mean that all human beings are related to the Elohim. This means that all humans have God as part of their nature. They have "God in us," and the Planet Earth is truly a God-directed global village.

It is certain that Yahweh Elohim had considered the likely effects the Randy 96K would have upon the earth's population in this scenario. Perhaps He wanted all 7.5 billion (2017 figure) humans living on earth to be related to the Elohim, His creation. He would have His reasons, and we could speculate about them, but we cannot know with any certainty what His reasons are. Perhaps His reasoning is related to the long-awaited "end times." If we are waiting for the period of Lucifer's rule to end, we could be waiting for another 165,000 years before the long-awaited official return to earth of AC so that he can receive the Planet Earth as his gift from Yahweh Elohim, as was originally intended.

<hr />

There are likely to be numerous combinations and permutations of variables affecting all imagined scenarios, but trying to decipher them would be beyond boring. So, we will leave it at just two scenarios, as outlined above. We need to consider our friend Lucifer for a bit, because the circumstances there have a direct bearing on all of us.

The churches, Christian and others, have painted Lucifer as the ultimate evil: the devil, Satan the Adversary. However, Yahweh Elohim named him Lucifer—the Morning Star, the Shining One—and our Yahweh Elohim is omniscient. Perhaps our Yahweh Elohim saw, apart from the grandeur of such an exalted one, one of the *first* of his kind, the potential for great love, compassion, consideration, and respect.

The churches, just like our society's politicians in general, need an adversary as a distraction for us, their poor benighted citizens, and as a foil to keep our eyes away from their avarice, duplicity, and savagery.

Politically and conflict-wise, after the First World War, we had Hitler and the Nazis, which led to the Second World War. After the Second World War, we had Stalin, Communist Russia, and the Cold War, then Mao Tse-Tung, with Communist China backing North Korea and the Korean

War. Then, we had Ho Chi Minh and the Vietnam War, and now the various conflicts in the Middle East.

This is the legacy of the distractions our politicians bestow upon us to facilitate the production of war materials to fight all those conflicts; the financial rewards of which line the pockets of the perpetually hungry and eternally greedy. Much slaughter and destruction results from their hunger and greed. Greedy humans financially line their pockets, but destructive Elohim forfeit their everlasting life—Yahweh Elohim revokes their immortal status, and they eventually die.

The situation is not appreciably different with the churches, particularly the so-called Christian churches. From the earliest times after Jesus's death, the leaders of the Christian church were rapacious. The acquisition of power and wealth was their motivation, not unlike the politicians of all ages. The so-called preaching of the gospel of the coming kingdom of God is merely an excuse, a justification for their church's existence, which feeds their greed. Evidence of their savagery is clear in the Inquisition. Their greed is seen in the acquisition of trillions of dollars sequestered away in real estate worldwide, not to mention the Catholic Church's financing of businesses, ranging from owning and financing tractor manufacturing concerns, to condom production and international banking.

How did we arrive at this juncture?

CHAPTER 4

THE JEWS AND THE ESSENES

We arrived at this juncture because of the life of Jesus Barsabbas—or AC, the label I have given the Elohim Jesus throughout much of this story. The centaur is an ancient Greek mythological creature with the head, arms, and chest of a man, and the lower body and legs of a horse. The choice of such a mythical creature may show Jesus's appreciation of all mythology and his acknowledgement that he, a dual star, may be the third-brightest star in his firmament. Or, he might just have liked the sound of the two words together.

It was felt to be important to hide AC's identity. He was personally named Jesus by our One, and so the use of the name Jesus would have been entirely appropriate. However, the readers of this story are twenty-first century dwellers who might be distracted by the name Jesus and all that name suggests.

To understand Jesus the Essene, we must first understand his people, the Jews, and their religion, Judaism. It has often been said that Jesus was a typical Jew of his day. This is incorrect. He was anything but typical, as we shall learn as this story unfolds.

Then, as today, the Jews and Judaism were divided into factions. Some of the better-known factions of that time were the Pharisees, the Sadducees, the Zealots, and the Essenes. Jesus was born into the Essene sect. Yet, Christianity never seems to publish this little-recognised fact about the life and origins of Jesus, perhaps because the Essenes were viewed as a fringe element of Judaism, not quite belonging, and lacking power. Naturally, because Jesus was born into the Essenes, we need to appreciate the ascetic nature and ultrastrict lifestyle of the Essenes, and how and where Jesus fitted into this form of Judaism. We also need to appreciate why Jews, Essenes, and Gentiles were prepared to forsake their former faiths and, instead, to love and follow Jesus.

<hr/>

We shall discuss the Jews first. Many Jews, then and now, believe that the Jewish nation is a "special people," a "chosen people" set aside by God. They believe that they have a special relationship with their God, who communicated directly with the Jewish leaders of ancient times and made covenants with them. For example, according to the Torah, the first of the three Jewish patriarchs Abraham, was the father of two tribes of peoples: Arabs, through Hagar and Ishmael; and Israelites, though Sarah and Isaac. Isaac, married to Rebekah, was the second patriarch, and the third was Jacob, who was married to Leah. The period of Abraham's life and times is unknown. So, the existence of these patriarchs, their lives and their accomplishments, are passed to us and the Jews verbally by oral tradition. There are few written accounts of those times, but the epic of Gilgamesh is one rare written story of the time available to us.

There are plenty of accounts in the Bible and elsewhere of the One the Jews presumed was Yahweh Elohim, or their Lord God, supposedly speaking to various people. For example, God is supposed to have spoken in a vision to Abraham and told him of the covenant between God and Abraham. God tested Abraham's obedience by ordering him to sacrifice his son Isaac, and Abraham proved his obedience to God; however, God spared Isaac.[5]

We again see the perceived special relationship between the Jews and their God in the description of the exodus from Egypt. This involves the Jews, the twelve tribes of Judah, escaping from Egypt by what appears to be supernatural means (that is, either the death angel or a virus slew the Egyptians, but not the Jews.) Followed by the Jews' exodus out of Egypt in about 1446 BCE, was another seemingly supernatural event where the waters of the Red Sea parted so that the Jews could walk from Egypt to Sinai on damp, if not dry, sand. Once the Jews had crossed safely, the sea returned, engulfing Pharaoh's Egyptian army, and all were drowned. The Jews went on, unscathed.

Moses led the Jews into the Sinai wilderness where they wandered, seemingly aimlessly, for some forty years, until

---

[5] Abrahamic covenant: The voice of the Lord came to Abram in a vision and repeated the promise of the land and descendants as numerous as the stars. Abram and God made a covenant ceremony, and God told of the future bondage of Israel in Egypt. God described to Abram the land that his offspring would claim: the land of the Kenites, Kenizzites, Kadmonites, Hittites, Perizzites, Rephaims, Amorites, Canaanites, Girgashites, and Jebusites. (Genesis 15:1–21)

they espied the promised land, Palestine (or Israel, as it's called today) and eventually entered the land they believed their God had promised them. Moses, however, was not allowed to enter the promised land.

Moses, during their forty years of wandering, had received the Ten Commandments and assembled the first five books of the Bible, the Torah, or Pentateuch: the book of Genesis, the book of Exodus, the book of Leviticus, the book of Numbers, and the book of Deuteronomy. The books of Genesis and Exodus, particularly, were assembled from oral traditions, based on legends passed by word of mouth. The legend of the Great Flood where Noah and his family were saved, and Noah led the world's animals two by two onto his ark, is an oral tradition recounted by Moses in Genesis 6–9.

In the Australian Broadcasting Commission's television documentary *Riddle of the Dead Sea Scrolls,* Professor Barbara Thiering of the University of Sydney and certain theological critics label these oral traditions and the events they describe as myths—or, more accurately, "pious myths," as described by one commentator. They also describe the miracles that are attributed to Jesus as pious myths, and we shall examine those myths as we proceed.

These oral traditions and later written accounts would have us believe that the Elohim—or God or Yahweh Elohim or the Lord God—spoke to Moses out of a burning bush and gave him the Ten Commandments. Yahweh Elohim, or the Lord God, was supposed to have spoken to Abraham in a voice that could be heard and described to him the land He promised to Abraham—the promised land—and also described His covenant with Abraham. These instances where Moses and Abraham spoke directly with God (Yahweh

Elohim, or the Lord God) have been chosen to illustrate a point, because they are well known.

Moses and Abraham may have been powerful figures within the traditions of Judaism, yet they are still just men, like you, and I, and all the rest of us humans. Has God— Yahweh Elohim, or the Lord God—spoken to you in a voice that you could hear? Probably not. Those claiming that they have heard the voice of a god or the Lord God are delusional, in my opinion, despite their exalted status in the Bible.

I realised that I'm making a big thing of this, perhaps even blowing it out of proportion. But when we are dealing with religious beliefs, all sorts of claims can be, and often are, made that are based upon the most spurious of evidentiary support. People's religious beliefs are often based upon faith, and faith is "the evidence of something hoped for yet not seen," as the New Testament puts it. Yet, those claims are believed in good faith by the adherents of that religion, Judaism in this case, but Christianity too. The claims are added to the Bible and become divine right. It's not a purposeful lie, more like wishful thinking. But I'm convinced that there are many purposeful lies in the Bible, and we will be discussing them in this story too.

One of the pivotal purposeful lies centres around the true, powerful *gospel* that Jesus himself proclaimed, and not the watered-down pablum foisted upon us by the Christian churches. We will discuss this more fully in later chapters as well.

Firstly, before we consider anything else, we need to understand who the Essenes were and some of the peculiarities of the Essene sect of Judaism. This is important because Jesus was born and raised in an Essene household and lived as an Essene until he began his ministry at about the age of thirty.

Sources say that in 1946–47, one or two Arab shepherd boys found a cave near the archaeological ruins of Qumran, holding 981 manuscripts, some of which were previously unknown and unread hand-written scrolls. Some of the manuscripts were stored in canopic jars and were in excellent condition, though many others were unsealed, fragmentary, and in a very poor state. These scrolls were authored by Essene scribes whose monastery at Qumran was located at the north-west corner of the Dead Sea, in the Judean wasteland or wilderness, about fourteen miles east of Jerusalem, as the crow flies.

The Essenes were the third-largest sect of the Jews who existed from about the second century BCE until the first century CE, during the period of Solomon's second temple. Essenes lived in most towns and cities throughout Palestine, but the monastery at Qumran and the township of Mar Saba were regarded as the main centres of the Essenes in Palestine.

In fact, the Essenes were an ultrastrict, ascetic, monastic order of monks who had been excluded, expelled, and exiled from mainstream Jewish life in Jerusalem by other pious Jews more powerful politically than the Essenes. So, to distinguish themselves from orthodox Judaism, the Essenes set up a society that paralleled, in almost every detail, the orthodox society and religion in Jerusalem. They set up their society at Qumran, where they located their monastery, and a secondary site at Mar Saba, some seven to eight miles away, on the way to Jerusalem. The Essene monastery at Qumran was called the "new Jerusalem"; it contained a "new temple," a "new holy of holies," and a "new priesthood."

There were very strict rules governing every aspect of the lives of the celibate monks of Qumran. Those rules were recorded in the scrolls found in the caves near Qumran, in the 1940s (as mentioned above). Eventually, eleven caves in all yielded valuable, unread scrolls. The title of some of the scrolls were The Manual of Discipline, or the Community Rule; The Temple Scroll; The War Scroll; and The Copper Scroll. Those scrolls record every aspect of the highly regulated, celibate lives of the Essene monks.

As one early commentator stated, "They lived without women, without love and without money."

The Essenes appear to have been quite secretive and tried to disguise the identities of such personages as the high priest, the Levites, and even Joseph, Jesus's father, for example. This was possibly done for security purposes. The Essenes, if not quite outlaws, were viewed as a somewhat dangerous, renegade sect to be watched. In this context, the spoken word could insidiously be taken out of context, misconstrued, and then used against the person for disciplinary purposes by the ruling hierarchy in league with Rome, the occupying power, in Jerusalem.

Almost everything about the Essene teachings and rituals had at least two layers of meaning. This was called the *pesher*, or *pesharim*, meaning, in the Hebrew language, "interpretation" or "solution."[6] For example, later, during Jesus's ministry, he told his disciples, in effect: "To them [meaning the ordinary people: ordinary Essenes and Jews] the 'Word of truth' is given in parables and stories, but to you the 'Word' is given and spoken plainly." Thus, for example, when the Essenes talk about a fig tree being planted in a vineyard, the vineyard is Judaism, and the fig tree may be Jewish members of the Asian, Greek, and Mesopotamian diaspora. There are many examples like this throughout the New Testament, and other examples will make this much clearer when we discuss the miracles of Jesus.

Expanding upon this notion of the *pesher*, or *pesharim*, we find that, not only was it used to disguise the identity of ranking officials within the Essenes, but it was also used to give those ranking officials a level of assumed power. For example, the Essenes believed that the person of the high priest, when performing his priestly duties, took on the identity of an Elohim, or even Yahweh Elohim Himself. The following quotation from Professor Thiering's book gives us some idea of how the *pesharim* was used:

> They developed under platonic influence a concept that the spirits and angels of heaven stood over them in the places where they worshipped, and entered into them to give them the authority they needed. A doctrine of incarnation was developed, and carried to the point of calling the

---

[6] The *pesharim* give a theory of scriptural interpretation, previously partly known, but now fully defined. The writers of *pesharim* believe that scripture is written on two levels: the surface, for ordinary readers with limited knowledge; the concealed one, for specialists with higher knowledge.

> priests and levites by the names of heavenly beings. As Philo shows, the high priest could be defined as a superhuman being, and in Jn 10:34-36 shows, some Jews could call themselves 'elohim, "Gods". Other priests were held to be the incarnations of angels or spirits, and these words were used by the human priest in the scrolls. Two leading priests and two leading Levites were called archangels, with the names Michael, Gabriel, Sariel and Raphael; and the names of their order were set down in the War Scroll.[7]

Two examples of the use of pseudonyms relate to the Levite who represented or assumed the power of the Archangel Gabriel. The Archangel Gabriel is usually identified as the spokesman for Yahweh Elohim, and it was Gabriel who announced to Mary and Elizabeth that they each would become pregnant and bear a child.

In Mary's case, the child was to be Jesus, the kingly Messiah of the Jews; it was prophesied that a "virgin" would conceive a child by the "Holy Spirit." (This prophecy will be discussed in much greater detail later in this story.)

Elizabeth, married to Zacharias, is described as "barren," and Archangel Gabriel announced that she would also conceive, in her advanced years, and bear a child.

In both these cases, the Archangel Gabriel would probably have been, as the quotation above from Professor Thiering's book suggests, a highly placed Essene Levite who assumed the mantle of the Archangel Gabriel as part of his duties.

In Elizabeth's case, the announcement is generally seen

---

[7] B. Thiering, *The Qumran Origins of the Christian Church*, 31–32.

as a miracle until one understands that Elizabeth was barren and had no children not because she could not conceive a child, but because her husband was living as a celibate monk at the monastery of Qumran and would not have sexual relations with his wife.

In Palestine, most Jewish girls married young and raised families relatively early in their married life; this was also the case among the Essenes. Elizabeth was older than the normal age for childbearing but still young enough to bear a child. Her child became John the Baptist, the priestly Messiah.

In the Essene sect of Judaism, many of the males were monks, and many of the females were nuns, and all of these were celibate. However, certain of the monks were required to marry to ensure the continuation of important familial blood lines. Joseph may have been a humble carpenter, but he was also born of the direct line of King David, and, thus, he was required to marry to maintain the royal lineage of King David. (As mentioned above, the announcement of the conception and birth of Jesus, which is very interesting, will be discussed later in this story.)

In conclusion of this brief section relating to the Essenes, there is an interesting point to note. The Essenes had a peculiar view of the natural order of the world. They conceived that there were three levels of existence: the heavens above, where, presumably, the Lord God (Yahweh Elohim), the angels, and the heavenly host resided; hell (or Hades) below, where sinners suffered; and, between heaven and hell, there was earth. However, the earth was flat.[8]

---

[8] According to Google, the Flat Earth Society still exists today *https://en.wikipedia.org/wiki/Modern_flat_Earth_societies*

CHAPTER 5

JESUS, THE ORIGINS OF CHRISTIANITY, AND THE BIBLE

Now, how does this relate to Jesus and the foundations of Christianity?

It was announced by an angel—again, probably a Levite posing as the Archangel Gabriel—that a "virgin" (the Virgin Mary, mother of Jesus) would conceive a child by the Holy Spirit and become pregnant. It was announced that Mary, though unmarried and still a "virgin," would give birth to Jesus, who would become the prophesied kingly Messiah to the Jewish nation and then lead the Jewish nation to cleanse Palestine and, eventually, all the world of the "sons of darkness."

Looking at this prophecy from a different perspective, it is one of the founding, central tenants of the Catholic Church that Mary, a "virgin," would conceive and become pregnant by the Holy Spirit and have a child by an "immaculate conception." The birth would be normal and natural; only the conception would be by supernatural means. After the birth of Jesus, Mary would remain a perpetual virgin and would have no more children.

—————◇◆◇————

Various Gospels in the New Testament record that Jesus was born in Bethlehem during a census conducted by the Romans. More may be said about this, but Jesus wasn't born on December 25, nor was he visited by the Three Kings—the Three Wise Men, or Magi—at his birth. These are pagan myths. (We will discuss more about myths, even pious myths, later.)

Jesus grew up in Nazareth, where his father, Joseph Barsabbas, worked as a carpenter. As has already been established, Jesus's parents were members of the Essene sect of Judaism, and Jesus, as a child, was raised in the Essene tradition. Also, as mentioned, Joseph was of the direct lineage of King David, and so he was viewed as an important member of the Essenes and often had to travel from Nazareth to Qumran to attend important religious functions there. During the times that Joseph's position required him to be in Qumran, Jesus and his mother would stay at Mar Saba, which, as an adjunct to the monastery at Qumran, had places where nuns and the families of personages like Joseph could stay. Mar Saba, as previously described, is situated about halfway between Qumran and Jerusalem.

Again, since Jesus's genealogy shows that he was born into the royal line of King David, the Essenes expected him to become their kingly Messiah. This, of course, is a quandary for biblical scholars, as Christianity (read: the Catholic Church) holds that Jesus was fathered by the Holy Spirit, but then, how could he be the kingly Messiah of Davidic lineage?

Jesus was baptised by John the Baptist, suggesting that, initially at least, Jesus had been a follower or disciple of John. The followers of John the Baptist were called "sons of light" and all others the "sons of darkness." John was critical of Pharisees and Sadducees, other sects of Judaism, and preached a strict doomsday message of "the kingdom of heaven is at hand" and a "coming judgement." Some two thousand years later, the message delivered by certain preachers and churches is essentially the same.

The two Messiahs—kingly and priestly—were to cleanse Palestine of all sons of darkness. In fact, the whole world was to be cleansed of the sons of darkness, meaning that the Romans would be expelled from Palestine, and, eventually, the Jews would rule the entire world. This, of course, was a fanciful, delusional idea, but it was widely held by many Jews, particularly the Zealots (a rebellious sect).

As he grew into manhood, Jesus's life and mission (or ministry) developed differently from John the Baptist's. John adhered to the strict, ascetic life of the Essenes, but Jesus, perhaps seeing those rules as unimportant and unnecessary, opposed the strictures and rules of the Essenes. Thus, followers of Jesus—Christians, as they came to be called— were labelled "seekers after smooth things."

Jesus was more a social reformer than strictly a religious activist, as his contemporary, John the Baptist, appears to have been. However, Jesus opposed those who sold baptism for money: a half shekel for baptism. He also opposed the selling of forgiveness of sins for money, and, consequently cast out the money changers from the temple—that is, the Qumran "Jerusalem temple," not the real Jerusalem temple in Jerusalem itself.

Jesus also allowed married men and women, and Gentiles, to partake of the communal meals and the holy meals. This was strictly forbidden in Essene society and even in the broader Jewish society as well, and there was much opposition to Jesus and his followers for this controversial "way" that eventually lead to his crucifixion.

After watching the ABC documentary: *The Riddle of the Dead Sea Scrolls*[9], and, later, after reading Professor Thiering's book *The Qumran Origins of the Christian Church,* I began to gain an understanding of the foundations of first-century Christianity and even, to some extent, Christianity today. It became clear to me that Christianity today has little to do with the man Jesus and his message of love, tolerance, and inclusion. To the best of my knowledge and understanding, there are no groups and no churches on this beautiful blue-green Planet Earth that can truly be called Christian today, in the sense of the church that Jesus founded.

⚊⚊◈◆◈⚊⚊

I think we need to recognise some salient arguments about the Bible. The King James Version of the Bible is called the Authorised Version. There are Catholic versions (Douay-Rheims and others), Protestant versions, Jewish versions, and contemporary versions. Essentially, all adherents to their respective versions of the Bible claim it to be the "inspired word of God." But, just as argued earlier, that you and I have never heard the voice of God ourselves, neither did the personages who appear in the Bible.

Figures like Moses, Abraham, Isaac, Jacob, and all the

---

[9] Wikipedia: *https://www.youtube.com/watch?v=Vkhqd0xVejg*

rest, might all very well be exalted figures worthy of our respect and admiration, but that doesn't mean they heard the voice of God speaking to them. You and I and everyone else are all ordinary humans, and if none of us have heard the voice of God, then neither did they.

I realise that this is not a very compelling argument. But, 5,000-odd years later, it's very easy to add this paragraph or sentence to the Bible, or to omit that sentence—who would ever know? Particularly, if the scriptural additions or subtractions bore the imprimatur of the Catholic Church. This argument sounds cynical, I know, and will be rejected outright by Bible scholars and all Christian religions out of hand, but they have a vested interest in maintaining the status quo.

The whole idea of the Bible being the inspired word of God is a controversial topic, and one I am not eager to engage. The proponents of the various versions of the Bible all believe and consider that the version they espouse is the inspired word of God. Their consideration is based upon the Bible itself, which holds that it is the inspired word of God. This then becomes a circular argument, with the adherents of the various versions of the Bible holding that it is "God breathed" or "inspired," based upon the Bible's claim that it is "inspired by God."

Some hold that the Bible is inspired by God because of what is predicted—or prophesied—and what has come true in the past. Some Christian churches are adamant about the veracity of the Bible, based upon the accuracy of its predictions. But, one could easily ask, What predictions have come true? And, in my opinion, one will never receive a satisfactory reply.

The Bible is beautiful literature. The poetry is divine, and the history recorded in the Bible is reasonably accurate. I have been informed that during the First World War, certain allied leaders used the Bible to identify the location of oases and waterholes, but that doesn't mean that every word of the Bible is inspired and infallible. According to the Catholic Church, the Pope is infallible under certain specific circumstances (or so the church claims). Does that mean he's infallible? I don't think so, but the Catholic Church would disagree with me.

The divinity of Jesus the Risen Christ and the divinity of the Christian church are related subjects. The divinity of the church is assumed and rests upon the divinity of Jesus Christ. The divinity of Jesus the Christ rests upon the biblical account of the circumstances of his miraculous birth, his life, the miracles he performed while he was alive, the circumstances of his cruel death by crucifixion, his resurrection, and his ascension to heaven. These issues will be addressed in the next chapter.

<hr />

As an aside, this is my story, as I've made clear from the beginning. I've tried to avoid using *I* and the *me* as much as possible. However, I must assert my view here. In my opinion, despite the apparent endorsement of it by the Ones, this system sucks!

I'm still typing, so I haven't been struck down dead—at least, this time. *A-a-a-agh!*

Fooled you! I'm still here typing.

But who would ever vote for a system that means the moment you are born, you have a death sentence hanging over your head, like some sort of supernatural sword of Damocles?

Obviously, someone who didn't have to, or wasn't required to, participate in such a system.

For a while, like everyone else, I saw Lucifer as the bad guy. I thought he must have designed the system we live and die under. But now I'm not so sure. Perhaps, the seven Ones agree about this, and in their exalted wisdom, they might see the present system as the best system. As Albus Dumbledore said, "The next great adventure is death." But who wants to die?

I've got a better system—sorry, O exalted Ones. My system takes death out of the equation. At a time of our choosing, provided we have addressed all our faults and flaws, we step onto a desculator that takes us to another universe and another One, for a working holiday before returning home. No death, illness, sickness, incurable lurgy, and we get our passport stamped by the new One to show we are worthy.

My system may take a little tweaking. I'm working on it.

CHAPTER 6

THE DIVINITY OF JESUS AND THE CHRISTIAN CHURCH

In this story, a storyline could have been proposed that talks about Elohim and Yahweh Elohim, and in the context of Christianity it would make sense to very few. Yet the precursor church, some two thousand years ago, which became the modern Catholic (Christian) Church of today, believed and proposed that Jesus is the Christ who was born of a "virgin" by an "immaculate conception"; who later died on the cross; who rose from the dead after three days in a tomb; who ascended into heaven and now sits at the right hand of the Father, together, with the Holy Spirit or Spigot, following the malapropism of Roan Atkinson, playing the part of the trainee priest in the movie *Four Weddings and a Funeral*).

Essentially, the evidence for the divinity of Jesus is his performance of supposed miracles, along with the so-called gospel of the kingdom of God that he preached, which ultimately led to his crucifixion and then the fantasy of his so-called resurrection from the dead and all its attendant happenings.

Earlier in this story, the Essene practice of using the *pesher,* or *pesharim,* was briefly introduced. According to Professor Thiering, "the *pesharim* give a theory of scriptural interpretation, previously partly known, but now fully defined." The writers of *pesharim* believed that scripture is written on two levels: the surface level, for ordinary readers with limited knowledge; and the concealed level, for specialists with higher knowledge. Earlier, a quotation by Jesus himself made this clear when he told his disciples that to the ordinary Jews the meanings of certain events and happenings were told in stories and parables at a surface level, whereas to the disciples the second or deeper level was made known.

This is how all the miracles of Jesus need to be viewed, according to Jesus. A surface meaning for ordinary people, and a deeper meaning for Jesus's disciples and the other Essenes, who were not followers of Jesus but who would have understood the use of the *pesharim.*

So, let us look at the miracles associated with Jesus and those miracles that were, supposedly, performed by Jesus.

The *Immaculate Conception* and the *Virgin Birth*

In the Essene sect of Judaism, a girl remained a virgin until she married. Before marriage, couples considered to be courting observed two periods of time, totalling five years. The first was a betrothal period of two years, during which a girl might be betrothed to a man, but no sexual intercourse was permitted. If, after two years, the couple proved emotionally and psychologically compatible, there would be a second period—this time, of three years' duration—during which sexual intercourse was permitted. This second period was to see if the girl was fertile and able to have a child. Once her fecundity was established—that is, she could conceive and bear a child—the couple would marry. There was no divorce within the Essene sect. Once married, the girl was no longer considered a "virgin."

It appears that Mary, officially still a virgin (as described above), became pregnant with Jesus during the two-year betrothal period where no sexual intercourse was permitted. According to Essene practice, Joseph would have been within his rights to have Mary cast aside, but he did not do so. Thus, Jesus was conceived of Mary, still officially a virgin at that time. So, part of the prophecy appears to have been fulfilled.

According to the *pesharim*, Joseph, an important man among the Essenes because of his direct familial lineage to King David, was known among the Essenes as both Joseph and other names. Just as, for example, the Essene high priest might be identified as an Elohim, or even as Yahweh Elohim, in the performance of his priestly duties, so, too, in like manner, Joseph, Mary's betrothed, was known as the Holy Spirit.

Thus, a "virgin" conceived a child of the "Holy Spirit," in fulfilment of one of the prophecies. Jesus, however, was conceived and born by normal human means. There is nothing divine about his conception and birth. He grew up as a normal human boy, maturing into manhood, where he was a normal human man. No miracle in this case.

<hr />

The Catholic Church would have us believe that not only was the conception and birth of Jesus divinely instigated by an *improper conniption* (oops—I mean, *immaculate conception*) but also that Mary remained a virgin for the remainder of her days and had no more children. This is incorrect Jesus had four brothers—James, Joses and Judas, Simon—and, presumably, numerous sisters not mentioned in the scriptures.

All Essenes would have been familiar with the *pesharim* and aware of the circumstances of Jesus's birth. Ordinary Jewish and Gentile converts, however, might not have been aware of the *pesharim* and the dual layers of meaning. Just as you and I would have been unaware of the two levels of meaning unless informed and schooled in the *pesharim* by Professor Barbara Thiering.

The Changing of Water into Wine: The Marriage Feast at Cana in Galilee

There is much symbolism here, and the *pesher,* or *pesharim,* technique is required. The wedding feast was at Mar Saba, near Qumran, and not at Cana in Galilee, as described in the scriptures. It was, in fact, a run-of-the-mill parish council meeting.

The ceremony at Mar Saba was normally an entry point for parishioners to the foot-washing ceremony symbolised by the water, and that was all. By changing the symbolism of water into fermented wine, and not just the inferior-quality new unfermented wine, it allowed those who were previously considered unclean not only the right to enter the congregation, but also the right to advance two places, and to become ministers of the congregation.

Jews, particularly Essenes, were very exclusive at that time. You could not enter the congregation or participate in the sacred meals if you were viewed as unclean; hence the need for foot-washing or even baptism by full immersion in the Dead Sea. Married men who had intercourse with their wives could be viewed as unclean, and Gentiles were also seen as unclean. Jesus, by changing the symbology from water into fermented wine, was saying that anyone could become a priest, not just Levites.

This is an example of Jesus's love, tolerance, and inclusiveness. The changing of the symbolism of the water into wine was not a miracle, per se, but, rather, an action by Jesus in direct contradiction to the exclusion and intolerance practised by the Jews—particularly, the Essenes. As Professor Thiering says, "A layman could be both Pope and a high priest."[10]

As you might already have begun to appreciate, this action by Jesus did not endear him to the Jewish, the Essene, or even the Roman authorities. Jesus could do these things because, within the Essene community, he was a man of stature. Many Essenes, Jews, and Gentiles were drawn to him through his message and obvious practice of showing love, tolerance, and inclusion. He was a direct descendant of the Jewish King David (on his father Joseph's side, as we have seen), and, as such, was seen by the Essenes as their kingly Messiah.

Feeding the Multitude

As with the so-called miracle of changing water into wine, there is much symbolism in feeding the five thousand, and the Essene *pesher*, or *pesharim*, technique is required to understand the levels of meaning contained within the event.

---

[10] B. Thiering, *The Qumran Origins of the Christian Church*, 174.

In this instance, the five thousand people are ordinary or lower-order parishioners, including circumcised Gentiles. The five barley loaves represented five newly ordained Levite priests, and the two fishes were two newly ordained Gentile priests—all of whom spoke to and taught the five thousand ordinary people, thereby feeding them with spiritual food.

The twelve baskets of crumbs gathered up stood for the ruling structure of twelve, who were lay ministers, and not twelve baskets of crumbs of bread.

Again, no miracle.

Walking on Water

In fact, the situation was prompted by a baptismal ceremony performed on the Dead Sea. Those individuals being baptised were seen as very unclean. They were required to be fully immersed in the saltwater of the Dead Sea, and then they were hauled out of the sea onto a boat. There was a Watergate into which the boat was sailed so that the crew and those who were baptised could alight from the vessel onto a jetty. Jesus walked along the jetty, situated above the water, to the Watergate to get onto the boat on which those who had been baptised were sitting. In that way, Jesus did not get wet like those who were baptised, yet he walked upon the water.

Again, no miracle.

Various Healings

The healing of the man with the withered hand stood for his permission to leave the celibate life and get married.

The healing of Jairus's "daughter" appears to be a reference to the healing of menstruous women following a ceremony where Jairus's daughter was "born" at the age of twelve.

According to Professor Thiering, the two episodes of "healing of the blind man" prefigured the conversion of Paul. Priscilla was the "crooked woman" who was to be promoted.

Raising Lazarus from the *Dead*

The word *dead*, in English, generally has one meaning: the person has expired and is literally deceased. Though, of course, there are colloquialisms where a person can be "dead to the world" asleep or "dead tired," and there are other exceptions as well.

In Hebrew, there are two words for the state of death or being dead. Thus, in terms of the *pesher,* or *pesharim,* technique, the word *dead* could have two meanings. The superficial level could mean that a person had died or expired. The deeper level of meaning, however, would have the Essene connotation, meaning that Lazarus had been disfellowshipped from the Essene community of monks, for some serious breach of Essene disciple. In this way, Lazarus was "dead" to the community of Essenes and was an outcast. The Essenes, to emphasise Lazarus's disfellowshipment, would clothe him in burial clothes and then place him in a tomb that was sealed by a large heavy stone. In the tomb, Lazarus, still alive, had minimal food and water—perhaps enough for three days. After three days, the Essenes would bring him out of the tomb and expel him from the community.

By raising Lazarus from his symbolic death, Jesus showed that he had forgiven Lazarus for his infraction or breach of Essene discipline. Jesus then allowed Lazarus to leave the tomb. In this way, Lazarus became a disciple and follower of Jesus.

The Crucifixion of Jesus

The accounts in the Gospels of Jesus's trial, torture, humiliation, and crucifixion appear to be quite accurate, according to accounts recorded in the Dead Sea Scrolls. After about three hours on the cross, we must assume that Jesus was given gall mixed with poison to drink, which Jesus first refused. Later, he was given vinegar with poison on a sponge to drink, and he drank some of it, because he was thirsty. Jesus's drinking of vinegar mixed with poison was suicide; an acceptable way of ending unendurable pain in the Jewish and Essene societies of the day. Jesus then appeared to have died. He was speared in his side; blood and water poured out, and he was pronounced dead. The two so-called thieves—Simon Magus and Judas Iscariot, who were Zealots and not thieves at all—had their legs broken so that they could not support themselves. Jesus and the so-called thieves were taken down from the crosses and placed in a nearby tomb at a place called Golgotha, the place of a skull. The tomb was owned by Joseph of Arimathea, a "rich man" and a disciple of Jesus.

Crucifixion was the Romans' preferred mode of execution. It is a very cruel and usually very slow form of execution. But, Jesus died quickly after taking the vinegar and poison, ostensibly committing suicide. The breaking of the legs of Simon Magus and Judas Iscariot meant that they, Jesus and the "thieves," could be taken down from the cross more quickly than might have been expected, so that the Sabbath day law would not be broken; it would have been a breach of the Sabbath day law to leave Jesus and the Zealots on their crosses.

In the tomb, despite their broken legs, the two Zealots forcibly administered a large dose of aloes mixed with myrrh to Jesus. The purgative effects of the aloes and myrrh worked on Jesus, and he expelled (vomited up) the unabsorbed poison and then began to recover. The Zealots must have been in great pain, but one of them managed to partially roll aside the large circular stone blocking the entrance to the tomb and quietly got the attention of the women in the wadi below the tomb, to let them know that Jesus was alive. There were still guards on the flat area of the hill above the tomb, near the crucifixion site, who might have alerted the authorities if they knew that Jesus was still alive in the tomb. The women below, including Martha and the two Marys (Jesus's mother, and Mary Magdalene, who later became Jesus's wife) had a litter made, and they pushed it through the narrow opening and into the tomb. Jesus was placed on the litter, and once the rock sealing the tomb was fully rolled back, Jesus was removed and carried away to the abbey of Mar Saba, halfway between Qumran and the real Jerusalem. The rock was later replaced, and the tomb resealed after the Zealots were carried away, so that no one would immediately know that the tomb was empty.

The voicing of the miracle of Jesus's death and resurrection started soon after Jesus was revived and taken from the tomb. I hadn't realised this until I reread a portion of Professor Thiering's book. I thought that the miracle of Jesus's supernatural healing and his being raised from the dead came much later, perhaps a hundred years or more after Jesus died naturally. The following excerpt from the Professor Thiering's book will explain:

> Simon Magus had now seen what he must do. He could be saved and gain enormous prestige, if he claimed that his powers had actually brought Jesus back from the dead. He had appeared to be dead on the cross, and Simon had only to confirm this on his medical authority and claim that he had been revived by supernatural means. If Peter, in particular, was convinced of this, he would try to save Simon, for Peter was willing to help Judas, but was against Simon. Helena was with the three women, and saw quickly what could be made out of the ambiguity of "he is risen from the dead". Simon told them to give the message to the disciples, and especially Peter. He added that they would be able to see Jesus in "Galilee", Mar Saba and Mazin, and this would confirm that a miracle had taken place.[11]

According to Professor Thiering, Jesus was later secretly taken up north to the Cana area of Galilee, where he was able to recover, rest, and recuperate from the ordeal he had suffered. In Cana, he was safe, away from the Essene and Jewish authorities who had tried to kill him and who might have tried again if they knew that he was still alive. It was noted that Jesus was physically affected by the poison he drank and remained in the permanent care of two physicians for the remainder of his days.

Again, according to Professor Thiering, there are accounts of Jesus preaching to the Jewish diaspora and

---

[11] B. Thiering, *The Qumran Origins of the Christian Church*, 222.

Gentiles in Asia Minor, in Greece, in Rome, and in Europe. Professor Thiering hypothesises that Jesus lived in Rome and may, eventually, have died of old age there. Other sources suggest that Jesus, once he escaped from Qumran and the Essene community, did not remain celibate but married Mary Magdalene and, like his mother Mary and father Joseph, had children together.[12]

During the life and times of Jesus in Judea and Qumran, the miracles recounted in the New Testament were not miracles to Jesus's followers who knew him intimately. Anyone and everyone in Qumran and the wider Essene community would have known of the two layers of meaning to the occurrences, the so-called miracles. They would have known that five loaves and two fishes stood for people: five Levite monks, or loaves from Qumran and Gentile converts, or fishes. They would have known that Jesus walked on a jetty over the water to get to the boat, and the like.

I think we need to view the so-called miracles from the perspective of the early Christian church in the first, second, and third centuries AD. In the television documentary referred to earlier, Professor Thiering and most other scholars agreed that the miracles were myths—certainly, they do not appear in any of the historical commentaries of the time. One would expect that it would have become widespread knowledge if Jesus was performing many different miracles but, except for Josephus, whose account of Jesus's miracles is generally regarded by scholars as fraudulent, the historians

---

[12] It is documented in the Dead Sea Scrolls that Mary and Joseph had five sons—Jesus; James, or Jacob in Ephesus; Joses, called Joseph in Matthew 13:55; Jude, or Judas Barsabbas; and Simon—and numerous unspecified daughters. There goes women's lib!

of the time are strangely silent on the topic of miracles. Today, scholars remain largely silent, and there is certainly no consensus. There is a "sacred-ground effect" here. No one is prepared to examine the miracles. You don't prod a sleeping dog because it might jump up and bite you; it's better to just "let sleeping dogs lie," as the saying goes.

⋙◇◇◇⋘

Therefore, the divinity of Jesus rests upon the miraculous circumstances of his birth: that he was born of a *virgin* by means of an *immaculate conception* where he was fathered by the *Holy Spirit*. It also rests upon the numerous miracles that have been ascribed to him. It further rests upon the claim that Jesus was crucified and died as a result, was buried in a tomb for three days, after which he rose from the dead and ascended into heaven, where he now sits on the right side of God the Father, together with the Holy Spirit.

To have achieved those things, Jesus would have had to be more than human. He would have had to be divine. As a divine being, he could pay the price of our sins and reconcile us to our God "who art in heaven," as the Lord's Prayer begins.

If Jesus didn't fulfil all these things—or even any of these things—he would be classified as merely human, an ordinary, kind, loving, gentle, tolerant, inclusive human man, but certainly not the "Son of God" in any miraculous sense. He would not be any more, or any less, the son of God than you and I, too, are children of God.

Thus, the divinity of the Christian religion is assumed. It is assumed, based upon the purported divinity of Jesus the Risen Christ, that the Christian church is also divine. Without the divinity of Jesus, the Christian religion is simply a ritualised social gathering. It is a way of living in the world that intentionally harms no others—when it's run properly.

Numerous other similar organisations exist in the world, but they do not claim to be divinely based. Buddhism is a religion, with teachings, a philosophy of life, and a mentor, in the form of Siddhartha Gautama (the Buddha). There is the Jaina religion, whose leader was Mahavira (Mahavira) also known as Vardaman, the twenty-fourth *Tirthankara* (ford maker) of Jainism. There is Hinduism, considered the oldest religion in the world. Lord Krishna is one of the prophets of Hinduism. And, of course, there is Islam, with its prophet Muhammad.

Jesus Died for Us and Paid the Penalty for Our Sins

The original Christian church founded at the time of Jesus in Palestine, moved to Asia Minor, Greece, Rome, and Europe, following the crucifixion of Jesus, whilst Jesus was still alive. That church later created—or, perhaps, concocted—a doctrine that Adam and Eve's sin in partaking of the fruit of the Tree of the Knowledge of Good and Evil became what is now termed the "original sin." Therefore, because God told Adam and Eve not to partake of the fruit and they disobeyed and, therefore, sinned, you and I are held responsible for their so-called original sin. (Later in this chapter, I will discuss the Christian church's need for such a doctrine.)

The presence of original sin means that babies who die before they have been baptised already have the stain of sin on their souls and, thus, must spend time in *limbus infantium* or *limbus puerorum* (limbo) to pay for their part in the sins of Adam and Eve. Those of us baptised adults who die in a state of venial sin, who may recently have confessed our sins at a confessional before a priest, received absolution, and performed penance, may have to spend a short time in purgatory to pay for our past sins and, thus, to also erase the stains of sin from our souls. Of course, if we adults die in a state of mortal sin, then we are likely to go to hell and suffer the fires of hell, supposedly with Satan and his demons, for the rest of eternity, with no hope of remission. If you believe that doctrine of the church, it's rather scary. Of course, unlike us flesh-and-blood humans, Lucifer is able to take the form of pure spirit, which doesn't burn too well.

The trouble with sin is that we all do it every day, all the time (I'm using the royal we here and speaking for myself only, of course.) If we die in a state of original, venial, or mortal sin, we must endure punishment for our sins. The only way of avoiding punishment for our sins, whatever sins they might be, is to "wash ourselves in the blood of the Lamb"—or, to put it in layman's terms, to hand over responsibility for our sins to the redeeming act of Jesus, the Saviour, the Christ, the Anointed One, the Divine, who died on the cross for our sins and the sins of the world.

> In Christianity, the Christ (Greek word Χριστός, *Christos*, meaning "the anointed one") is a title for the saviour and redeemer who would bring salvation to the Jewish people and mankind. Christians believe that Jesus is the Jewish messiah called Christ in both the Hebrew Bible and the Christian Old Testament.[13]

It has been many years since I was involved with the

---

[13] Wikipedia; Wikipedia's entry for Christ.

Catholic Church. But, it is amazing how quickly the teachings of the church come back to mind. I was obviously very well-conditioned and indoctrinated all those years ago by the nuns of Saint Joseph's Convent at Lochinvar, where I attended fifth and six classes in primary school, and high school at the Marist Brothers in Maitland (until I was expelled and had to enrol in the Maitland Boys High School in East Maitland, to sit for my NSW Leaving Certificate [LC]).

I stated this earlier, but I will repeat it again here. If Jesus, the Lord, was born of a virgin (Mary) who had become pregnant by the Holy Spirit, an "immaculate conception," who performed all the miracles recounted above, was crucified, died, and was buried. If Jesus then rose from the dead, fully healed, and ascended into heaven to sit at the right hand of God the Father as part of the Holy Trinity, then the divine Lord Jesus could, I expect, rightly pay the penalty for our sins and the sins of the world.

The problem with that scenario is that Jesus was a man, a human being, and not divine. Therefore, we are left in a state of sin for all our lives and must either spend who knows how long in purgatory, or fry, crackle, and burn in the fires of hell for all eternity. You can see that the choices are limited, and none are appealing.

Later, where I try to analyse the various roles of the Elohim in our lives, you will see that I have concluded that each child born has a guardian angel, or guardian Elohim, to protect the child and, later, the adult throughout life. There may also be a resident or accompanying Elohim that experiences all the events and circumstances of being human, having to resist the machinations of our God-given free will, so that we eventually become perfected and able to attain nirvana, or enlightenment, and become a universal, pure spirit with, and like, Yahweh Elohim.

So, what is the role of sin in that arrangement? According to the Bible, sin is the breaking or transgressing of the law. The law refers to the Ten Commandments given by God to Moses on Mount Sinai, in the Judean wilderness, after the Israelites had escaped the Pharaoh of Egypt, along with all the other attendant laws of the Jews: clean and unclean foods, the keeping of the Saturday Sabbath, the Holy Days, and many more.

Please do not get me wrong; there is nothing wrong with the Ten Commandments. They are generally beneficial— serving God first, and mankind in a way that allows us humans to live together in a measure of peace and harmony ... a good thing. But I contend that the God who gave the Ten Commandments to Moses was not Yahweh Elohim, the Lord God of the universe, but rather the guardian Elohim of the Jewish people or nation. Just as children have a guardian angel or guardian Elohim, so, too, do nations; this is generally accepted by Christian religions.

So, what is Yahweh Elohim concerned about? He knows that we all sin and break the law; it's part of being human. I contend that He's not too concerned about that, though, obviously, I cannot speak for Him. He and the six other Ones are concerned about the fatal character flaws brought about by rampant ego and the wrongful application of free will. This has already been discussed in chapters 2 and 3; such situations will lead to fighting, upheaval, chaos, and destruction. The action of Lucifer in questioning Yahweh Elohim's decision to give Planet Earth to the Elohim Jesus as a reward is an example of ego run rampant, perhaps a temper tantrum. Lucifer was eventually ceded Planet Earth for one thousand years, but his temper tantrum exemplified the potential for a character flaw as a result of the gift of free will. Like human beings, Elohim are not robots.

You would think that, surely, the priests, bishops, and popes of the youthful Christian church, some two thousand years ago, would have recognised the importance of out-of-control ego, compared with missing mass on Sunday (a mortal sin of omission) or the venial sin of gluttony, or the venial sin of drunkenness, or the mortal sin of theft, and many more. Perhaps, the priests, bishops, and popes of the Christian church paid little heed to ego because they were so full of it themselves.

Rampant, unconstrained ego, derived from our free will, will lead to crimes against humanity by brutal people like Hitler, Stalin, and many others. So, why did the fledgling Christian church, in the early centuries two millennia ago, focus on doctrines concerning sins—relatively minor sins— when brutish men were responsible for murdering millions of humans?

The answer is relatively simple. When the church is responsible for the forgiveness of sins via a priest in a confessional, through the saving grace of Jesus the Redeemer who is in heaven, then the people are dependent upon the church and the priesthood for their spiritual well-being. A parishioner knows that he will be forgiven for getting drunk or hitting his wife. Parishioners know that after saying a few Hail Marys and a few Our Fathers—or maybe a few laps around the rosary beads, if the sin was really bad—then all will be forgiven, and all is well in heaven and on earth.

Yahweh Elohim's way is tougher, but much more effective,

against those brutish men responsible for wars, death, and plunder. Those brutes are born, they live their lives, they plunder, rape, and pillage for life after life after life, until, after multiple incarnations, they get tired of the incessant wheel of life and death revolving and revolving and start to develop some humanity. They begin to lose their ego, and start to be driven by love for humankind, animals, and Planet Earth, and they develop compassion and concern for humankind.

Yahweh Elohim's way may take longer than the Catholic Church's way of fostering dependency, but His way is more effective. After all, He has all the time in the world.

CHAPTER 7

Parallels between Christianity and Paganism

There are many parallels between Christianity and paganism. Christianity borrowed heavily from pagan religions and beliefs, possibly to make a foreign religion like Christianity appear more appealing to pagans who might potentially become followers. These parallels are basically myths—"pious myths," in the view of some commentators.

Here are some of the myths pertaining to Jesus:

- Jesus was the solar Messiah. In fact, he was regarded as the Essene's kingly Messiah of the House of David.
- He was born of a *virgin*, Mary, on December 25, in Bethlehem. In fact, Jesus was born in August or September, as the shepherds were still out in the fields tending their flocks when he was born. The weather is much too cold in December in Palestine for the shepherds to be out in the open at that time of year.
- Jesus's birth was announced by a star in the east.

- The Three Wise Men—the Magi, or the Three Kings—followed the star, to find the babe Jesus. The star in the east was Sirius and two other stars in a line pointing to Sirius. The three stars in line were known as the Three Kings.
- Jesus was a child teacher at twelve years old.
- Jesus was baptised by John the Baptist and then began his own ministry at thirty years of age.
- Jesus had twelve disciples.
- Jesus performed miracles: walked on water, turned water into wine, raised the dead, and healed the sick.
- Jesus was called the "True Son of God," the "Light of the World," the "Lamb of God," and the "Only Begotten Son of God."
- Jesus was betrayed by Judas Iscariot for thirty pieces of silver.
- Jesus was crucified, died, and was buried in a tomb for three days; he was then resurrected and ascended to heaven.

There are numerous parallels between the pious myths associated with Jesus and Christianity today and the myths pertaining to other gods. Some examples appear below.

Horus, circa 3000 BCE:

- Horus was born on December 25, to a virgin (Isis Mary).
- A star in the east announced his birth.

- He was adored by the Three Kings (the three stars in line).
- He was a teacher at twelve years old.

Attis, circa 1250 BCE:

- Attis was born of a virgin on December 25.
- He was crucified.
- He was dead for three days and was then resurrected.

Krishna, circa 3200 BCE:

- Krishna was born of a virgin.
- A star in the east signalled his coming.
- He performed miracles.
- After his death, he was resurrected.

Dionysus, circa 1500 BCE:

- Dionysus was born of a virgin, on December 25, in ancient Greece.
- He performed miracles (changed water into wine).
- He was referred to as "King of Kings," "God's only begotten son," and the "Alpha and Omega."
- On his death, he was resurrected.

Mithra

- Mithra was born of a virgin, on December 25, in Persia.
- He had twelve disciples.
- He performed miracles.
- On his death, he was buried for three days, and then he was resurrected.
- He was called "The Truth" and "The Light."
- He instigated Sunday worship.[14]

The pious mythic circumstances and events attributed to Jesus, and accepted by many Christians as applying to Jesus, were obviously adopted or co-opted by the leaders of the early Christian church from myths pertaining to other deities, along with the deeper level of meaning, the *pesharim*, within the Essene movement.

Professor Thiering describes this very well:

> Jesus, born to fight for a throne and an earthly kingdom, brought to it the one thing that was needed to transform it from a short lived political enterprise to an enduring society whose members saw further than nationality, or class, or any of the divisions that set one human being against another. The motive that accounts for his actions

---

[14] All the above accounts were sourced from a television documentary entitled *Zeitgeist*, which I viewed on DVD. *Zeitgeist*, part 1: The Deception of Christianity; part 2: The Conspiracy of the US Government and the Destruction of the World Trade Center in New York; and part 3: A New Consciousness (DVD 1:58; three-part DVD, Date of Release).

is that which has always been attributed to him: acceptance of all persons, without regard for social or physical barriers. He saw no one as clean or unclean, but Gentile as equal to Jew, slave as equal to freeman, female as equal to male. All were admitted into the sanctuary and into forms of ministry in the highest place. He gave himself wholly, abandoning his own privileges and offering his life to his friends. Although much about him remains unknown, even in the inner history, the personality that comes to light is in accord with what is known: that he was deeply loved, both by all who knew him, and by all who afterwards continued to call him Lord.[15]

Within Judaism, and Essene societies, Jesus had a very loving, tolerant, and inclusive message stating that we should all love one another, and which allowed the ritually unclean, women and Gentiles, access to the idea of one Lord God and the coming kingdom of God. One question that could be asked: Would Jesus's inclusive, tolerant message of love have survived his mortal death? Because the fact is that Jesus Barsabbas was mortal, a human like you and me. My feeling, in this superstitions world, is that without miracles, non-existent though they were, his message might not have survived. But I hope I'm wrong.

We look about us and see human organisations—government bodies, industrial firms, social organisations—and we can observe all the very human traits and frailties pertaining to the people in those organisations. There is always jockeying for power, attempts at heightening or

---

[15] B. Thiering, *The Qumran Origins of the Christian Church,* 156.

increasing prestige, backbiting, bad-mouthing, and lying. Why would it be any different within the Essenes and the early leaders of the so-called Christian church that developed after Jesus died? Jesus may have been a loving, kind, inclusive, tolerant human being whom people were drawn to and followed, but many of his followers were very human, filled with ego and all the character flaws and human traits and frailties of the majority of human beings.

Part of Jesus's attraction was his message, which, as I've said a number of times, was one of love, inclusion, and tolerance, and which was diametrically opposed to the attitudes that pervaded Judaism and the Essene sect. Gentiles, circumcised or not, were viewed as "unclean" and would never be fully accepted within Jewish—particularly, Essene—society. Certainly, they never would have been allowed into the priesthood. Not so with Jesus and his message, and that is the reason why Jesus's message was popular and widely accepted.

But what happened to Jesus's message after he died? There was encouragement to include Gentiles within the early Christian church because that increased membership meant increased power and money. However, within the church structure, all the human traits and frailties listed above, and more, still existed. This was the way it was in Judaism, within the Sadducees, the Pharisees, and the Essenes. Naturally, the jockeying for power and prestige continued within the early Christian church and up to this very day.

After all, we see all the human character flaws within many of the Elohim—Lucifer, for example. What happened to Lucifer, his helpers and the Randy 96K Elohim (my guesstimate) who came to earth? As one of the scenarios proposed earlier, they may still be here—ageless. Presumably, they can mate with humans, so that would mean that there are many generations of the offspring of the Elohim living among us. If a generation is of thirty years' duration, then there might be 6,667 generations of children of the Elohim living among us.

That is, potentially, a very large number of descendants of the gods. If each Elohim conservatively fathered three children in each generation, that would be 288,000 children directly fathered by the Elohim in the first thirty years. The number would grow exponentially every generation.

Lucifer is recorded in the Bible and all religions that believe in the devil see him as Satan, the Adversary who opposes Yahweh Elohim's works on Planet Earth. The emotive term "cast down," referring to Lucifer and his supporters as "cast-down" from heaven to earth by the Archangel Michael, when used in the biblical text, implies that Lucifer (whose name was changed to Satan) was compelled to leave Yahweh Elohim's heavenly realm. That seems unusually harsh and is, in fact, inaccurate. Lucifer may have had his faults and flaws, but Yahweh Elohim gave him dominion over Planet Earth for "a thousand years," knowing that experience would change him.

As discussed earlier, politicians and religious leaders everywhere must have an adversary to keep citizens' minds focused away from the greed and corruption of bad government and self-serving religion. So, too, it appears, the early writers and assemblers of the Old and New Testaments of the Bible had to have an adversary. Lucifer was ready-made. He was the ready-made "bogeyman" that everyone could hate.

I am not an advocate, apologist, or sponsor for Lucifer—he's an exalted spiritual being and powerful enough to take care of himself—but I consider that he has been badly and unfairly treated by all sides, particularly the Jewish and Christian religions.

How, then, might it be with "God in Us"?

CHAPTER 8

GOD IN US

I do not have a lot of trust in the accuracy of the Bible. Nevertheless, it is, perhaps, the only source of ancient historical writings readily available for use by the ordinary person. Unfortunately, it has too often been used by unscrupulous people for improper ends. I have criticised the Bible both for its frequently poor translations and contents passed to us through oral transmissions and oral traditions. For example, Genesis 1 and 2, the accounts of Noah and the Flood, and many other examples, cannot be verified historically or archeologically.

If there is a God—and I consider that there *is* a Lord God—then that Lord God would, most likely, have left us with some record of what has happened, even if it cannot be verified by direct evidence. Perhaps the Bible is that source from the Lord God.

Similar to my experience writing this story, Moses and his sources needed considerable imagination to come up with plausible biblical creation stories based on myths and legends that make sense and could, possibly, have occurred.

In 2 Timothy 2:15, we are told to "Study to show yourself approved unto God, a workman that needeth not to be ashamed, rightly dividing the word of truth." I expect that the phrase "... rightly dividing the word of truth" suggests that when we study, we should not simply accept the superficial meaning of a section of the Bible, but, rather, subject it to deeper scrutiny—perhaps, even to a form of the *pesharim*—so that a proper meaning might come forth.

When I first started studying the Bible at the Bible college I attended in the United States, one the scriptures that struck me as mind shattering was the one below, in John 10:34–36:

> Jesus answered them, "Is it not written in your law, 'I said, Ye are gods?' If he called them gods, unto whom the word of God came, and the scripture cannot be broken; Say ye of him whom the Father has sanctified and sent into the world, 'Thou blasphemest'; because I said, 'I am the Son of God'?"[16]

I have pointed this scripture out to numerous people. Many do not accept it, and, in fact, they usually deny it completely, almost getting angry at my contentiousness in bringing it to their attention. But here we have Jesus quoting a scripture from Psalm 82:6, which holds that we are gods.

Some 73 of the 150 Psalms are attributed to King David, but, apparently there is no hard evidence for that assertion.[17] Nevertheless, here we find a psalm in which the psalmist, whomever he or she was, is contending that we—you and I

---

[16] Psalm 82:6: "I have said, Ye are gods and all of you are children of the most High."

[17] Wikipedia; Wikipedia's entry for Psalms.

and Jesus—are gods. Where did the psalmist get the notion that "Ye are gods"? We are not told. But Jesus, in the context of a group of Jews—probably Essenes—wanting to stone him to death for supposed blasphemy, has used that quotation to justify that he, you, I, and, perhaps, even those angry Essenes, are all gods.

So, my claim is just that: we are gods—Elohim (or God, gods, or object(s) of worship) or descendants of the Elohim, with the blood of the Elohim flowing through our veins. If we are gods, as we have been called, presumably on another plane of existence, were we the Elohim gods) who created the heavens, the earth, the animals, birds, and fish, as well as men and women, under the auspices and direction of Yahweh Elohim, "the Lord God"?

Is there any evidence for this claim? Yes, I think there is.

At the start of this story, I suggested that Yahweh Elohim, our One of this universe (one of the seven universes created by the Big Bang and simultaneously by the seven subsequent singularities that poured forth the materials to build the galaxies, solar systems, and planetary systems) realised that the creation of our universe could not be just be a singular affair. Our One, and the other Ones, began to realise that the creation of their universes would be better, more fun, if there were other beings with each One, to help create those cosmic bodies. Those beings would, of necessity, be spiritual beings like the Ones themselves, but they would also have to be able to manifest in physical form. Our One felt, the more the merrier!

Firstly, our One created Michael then Lucifer, and then

He proceeded to create numerous other spiritual beings: Elohim, all of whom He named personally, setting tasks for them to do under the guidance of Lucifer and the other archangels He later created.

As we've already seen, the story unfolds with an Elohim who nicknamed himself AC (standing for Alpha Centauri) being given Planet Earth as his own pet project. He and friends he co-opted into helping him—all Elohim, or gods, like he was—set about to re-create the Planet Earth from the chaos that resulted from the aftermath of the singularity that started the creation process for our universe. AC, his friends, and our One called this Project Planet Earth. Eventually, animals, birds, fish, and vegetation of every description covered the entire Planet Earth, but the culmination of their efforts, after a couple of false starts, was the creation of males and females in the image of the Elohim; that is, in the very image of the gods themselves.

Today, we see human beings with different-coloured skin, different facial features, different eye shapes and colours, and many other differences. If there are Africans, Caucasians, Asians, Indians, Pygmies, Bushmen, and all the other diverse types of humans on Planet Earth, and if they, those humans, were created in the image of the Elohim, then the Elohim themselves must have originally been created in that diverse way by Yahweh Elohim, our One, the Lord God Himself. Obviously, as was suggested before, our Yahweh Elohim loves and wants diversity.

So, we find that Project Planet Earth is the first planet in all seven universes to be populated with human beings. It is estimated that the modern human variety, *Homo sapiens*, has been on this earth for about 200,000 years. As you already know, to celebrate this momentous feat brought about by AC and his friends, our One determined to give Planet Earth to AC and his friends as a reward.

Well, you already know about the ensuing disagreement between our One and Lucifer and that Lucifer was given stewardship over the earth for a thousand years. What emerged from the disagreement was the understanding that there is a potential flaw in the free-will personality and character traits of the Elohim, and that flaw could only be addressed by living a human life, or even series of human lives. It is understood that the spirit of the Elohim is largely fixed, immutable, and unchangeable. Human life, on the other hand, is almost infinitely changeable in a willing human subject. In this way, by living a human life, or multiple or successive human lives, the character flaw within the Elohim can be changed, moderated, and eliminated for good.

<hr />

To repeat what we have already discussed, two thousand years ago, we see the Elohim who nicknamed himself AC living on earth, in Palestine. His name was always Jesus, the name given to him personally by our One. On Planet Earth, his family name was Jesus Barsabbas. His mother and father were members of the Essene sect of Judaism. Jesus's father, Joseph Barsabbas, was of the familial line of King David, and I have heard that Mary may also have been of the royal line of Kind David. Jesus was expected by the Essenes to become their kingly Messiah. (You know the outcome.)

What needs to be considered now is that in Jesus Barsabbas we have the Elohim Jesus, who, with his friends, is responsible for the re-creation of Planet Earth and also for populating it with human beings created in the image of the Elohim (that is, the image of Jesus and his friends).

Think about it. We have the god who re-created Planet Earth, who subdued it, vegetated it, and stocked it with all sorts of life, including human life, now on Planet Earth himself, as a lowly human being and not as some great god who had the power to re-create an entire planet.

"Hold on now," you might say. "How do we know that the human person Jesus Barsabbas was really the Elohim Jesus— or AC, as he's been nicknamed?" You might then make the point that there could be millions of people with the name of Jesus on Planet Earth today, particularly in Spanish-speaking countries. How do we know there weren't hundreds of Essene Jesuses in Palestine two thousand years ago?

Well, the honest answer is that we don't know. But the Jesus in the New Testament of the Bible was schooled and confident enough to quote the scripture in John 10:34–36:

> Jesus answered them, "Is it not written in your law, 'I said, Ye are gods?' If he called them gods, unto whom the word of God came, and the scripture cannot be broken; Say ye of him whom the Father has sanctified and sent into the world, 'Thou blasphemest'; because I said, 'I am the Son of God'?"[18]

Anyone knowing enough of the scriptures to make that claim, and simultaneously finding the courage to do so whilst under the pressure of opponents who were gathering up

---

[18] Psalm 82:6: "I have said, Ye are gods and all of you are children of the most High."

stones to hoick at him, would have to be very switched-on. Jesus must have been a very charismatic person and very knowledgeable of the scriptures. Whilst, in principle, I would not claim that Yahweh Elohim spoke to him directly, Jesus was humble, likeable, magnetic, and charismatic enough for people to want to follow him. They even made a religion based upon his title—Jesus the Christ, the Anointed One—not necessarily his teachings.

So, I reckon that the Elohim AC/Jesus was the human Jesus of the New Testament.

An estimated 240,000 Elohim were initially created by our One in His quest to commence the creation process of a universe. One of these Elohim was Jesus, whom we find had returned to earth (at least once), about two thousand years ago and lived a "normal"—if that's what you wish to call it—human life in Palestine and, later, in Asia Minor, Greece, and Rome, where he probably died an elderly man, beloved by those who knew him.

What made Jesus special to those who knew him? Perhaps, he knew this story about the Elohim I have told you. He had many more resources than I have. He had the Jewish Pentateuch assembled by Moses and was schooled in reading the Pentateuch and any of the Dead Sea Scrolls—which, incidentally, the Essenes, his people, authored. It should be realised that Jesus would not need to translate Hebrew, his native tongue, and, perhaps, not even Attic Greek or Latin, as we present-day humans need to do. His readings would have been free of translation errors, unlike our Bibles today. He was immersed in the ethos of his day and would also have had other scriptural materials, such as the book of Isaiah, the book of Daniel, the book of Job, the Psalms—and many more, too numerous to name here—and, in all cases, he would have been able to read the original text without needing to translate. If Jesus, the Essene living on Planet Earth two thousand years ago, knew this story, or pieced it together and talked to others about it, as I am talking to you, he would probably have been viewed in one of at least two ways.

Firstly, Jesus might have been viewed as insane, "certifiable," and very dangerous. As an Essene, Jesus had all the tools he would need to "rightly divide the word of truth," and that might make him a direct threat to the powers that be within the Essene hierarchy, the Judaic hierarchy in Jerusalem itself, and even the Roman governor and the occupying forces of Rome.

But even if certifiably insane, he would still have garnered followers thrilled by his message that he and they—that is, those who accepted "the word of truth"—were originally Elohim and would return to being Elohim after their human lives were over.

In today's world, we have so many competing interests. We have television, radio, movies, sports matches, Olympic Games, horse racing. ... You get my point? None of these distractions were available to the conscientious Essenes, celibate monks who prayed all day and half the night. The only ways the Jews, Greeks, and Romans communicated was by oral messages or written text delivered by messengers on foot or, perhaps, horseback. The heliograph and Morse code came much later.

Jesus must have been a gifted orator with a powerful message, since he managed to assemble some five thousand people to hear him and five newly ordained Levite priests and two newly ordained Gentile priests speak, and, thus, feed them spiritually with a distinctive spoken message. What if his message was this: "Ye are gods"—as I am god, an Elohim, not just the "son of God"?

This, presumably, was the message that a group of Essenes had heard, and for which they were prepared to stone him to death for blasphemy. If Jesus had said, "I am a son of God" or "I am a child of God," that would have been a different situation; such statements were not unheard of in Essene or mainstream Jewish society. But to say, "I am god" was altogether another situation: it was blasphemy, a stoning offence.

In this day and age, with all our distractions, if I were to say, "I am god (an Elohim)," I would probably be completely ignored, or, perhaps, sent to a funny farm where all is green, and the rooms are small and padded.

Certainly, there would be no comment and debate by the so-called Christian church currently extant. There might be a few who read this book who will try to take me to task as a heretic defaming the Christian religion. They did that with Professor Thiering after the documentary aired on ABC TV on the Friday night before Easter in 1990. A large group of Christian ministers, and even some Jewish rabbis, as I recall, harangued her and castigated her for her research and her position regarding Jesus and the Christian church. But, officially, the churches—the Catholic Church, the Church of England, the Baptist Church, the Uniting Church, the Jehovah's Witnesses, the Seventh-Day Adventists, and so on—all were startlingly silent.

The fact is that the churches have all the time in the world.

Remember, you don't poke a sleeping dog; it might jump up and bite you. It's best to let sleeping dogs lie. Professor Thiering's research and books, which caused such a stir in the late 1980s and early 1990s, are now mostly forgotten—just as this book will be, if it's ever published.

Back to the ways that Jesus might have been viewed. Secondly, he might have been seen as a visionary with a message of truth that ordinary people could hear and accept. All sorts of people would have flocked to see him and listen to his message, which would have been very different from the pablum dispensed by the Essene leadership—and, later, of course, by the Christian church hierarchy. Hence, as in the previous example, Jesus would have been a serious threat to the powers that be.

Jesus's message was very inclusive, whereas the Essene and Judaic authorities were exclusive, prohibiting Gentiles and women from places of authority and service. Jesus's message was very tolerant of the differences between peoples; the polar opposite of the message preached by the authorities. To the followers of Jesus, his inclusive message stated that a slave was as good as his master and as good as any free-man. Women were as good as men and could hold positions of authority in the church. Gentiles were as good as Jews and could become priests and ministers. There was no such thing as uncleanness, as there was within Judaism, especially among the Essenes.

Whilst no one among the Essenes would literally have believed the tales about Jesus's miracles, the newer Gentile converts, outside of Palestine, unfamiliar with the Essene *pesher,* or *pesharim,* and the multiple levels of meaning it revealed, might literally have believed that the miracles attributed to Jesus were true and had actually happened.

As Christianity began to spread throughout Asia Minor, Greece, Mesopotamia (Iraq and Iran), Rome, and much of Europe, there were unscrupulous Essenes—Simon Magus, Helena, and others—who would use the false tales about Jesus's miracles to persuade newly converted Gentiles of Jesus's "immaculate conception" and the divinity it presaged, and then extrapolate that assumed divinity and extend it to the Christian church and its ministers and priests.

Jesus might have survived his crucifixion and time in the tomb, recovered, and gone on to live in Rome, married to Mary Magdalene and a father of children. But Jesus, a loving, caring, tolerant human man, could not be everywhere to combat the lies that unscrupulous so-called Christian ministers spread about him.

So, Christianity with its assumed divinity, based upon the presumed divinity of the ordinary—extraordinary, really— human man, Jesus, flourished and grew into the monolith it is today. Today's so-called Christian message about Jesus is still about his immaculate conception by the Holy Spirit, the miracles he performed later on, and, finally, his miraculous healing by Simon Magus after dying on the cross, and then rising and ascending to heaven where he, as part of the Holy Trinity, now sits at the right hand of God the Father, together with the Holy Spirit.

There is nothing in the message of Christianity, whether from its onset or today, about the fact of Jesus being an Elohim, beloved of Yahweh Elohim and eventually promised dominion over this Planet Earth, as Yahweh Elohim had originally intended. Also, there is nothing in the message of Christianity, with respect to the words of Psalm 82:6 and John 10:34–36, about any humans being Elohim in the same fashion as Jesus was an Elohim.

CHAPTER 9

--------~~~◇◇◇◇~~~--------

GOD IN US: ATTAINING ENLIGHTENMENT

Before heading off around India in late 1990 to do the guru circuit—to see Sathya Sai Baba at Puttaparthi; Papaji in Lucknow; perhaps Amma in Southern India; and Bhagwan Shree Rajneesh's ashram in Pune, south of Mumbai—I arrived in New Delhi to acclimatise. One night, I was having dinner with an American guy who called himself a *sannyasin* (whatever that means) and we talked about spiritual things. I didn't know much about enlightenment, but I have been told that Gautama Siddhārtha (the Buddha), Mahavira of the Jaina religion, Osho (formerly known as Bhagwan Shree Rajneesh), and others were regarded as enlightened masters. I asked my dinner companion whether he was enlightened. After a very brief falter, he told me he was. He seemed an ordinary guy to me, but what did I know?

My first stop on the guru circuit was at the Osho ashram in Pune. I intended to stay there for, perhaps, less than a week, before heading south to see Sai Baba. But, as it turned out, I stayed there for the entire year that I was in India. I didn't get to see any of the other masters.

After a brief time, I became a sannyasin, and I began to love Osho. Before coming to the ashram, I hated him, but whilst at the ashram, I saw a different person in the video discourses played each night in the Buddha Hall at Pune and in the hundreds of books transcribed from his discourses. I never saw him in person whilst he was alive (he died on January 19, 1990), but there was something compelling about him that I couldn't define. He said he became enlightened on March 21, 1953, when he was in his late teens or early twenties, and I accepted that. He discoursed on his enlightenment in his book, *The Discipline of Transcendence,* volume 2. He was certainly extraordinarily intelligent.

If Osho were alive, and someone asked whether he thought that Jesus was an enlightened master, I feel certain that he would say yes. After all, Osho himself named one of the buildings in the ashram after Jesus. However, the most imposing structure at the ashram, during my time there, was the Buddha Hall, which included a huge marquee and a vast white marble floor. Osho obviously loved Buddha and discoursed widely on him. I do not think that Osho was impressed with the face of Christianity in the world today, but the man Jesus was an entirely different matter.

My labelling of Jesus as an enlightened master would be based on more than mere opinion or the fact that a religion, Christianity, was named for him. My firm acceptance of Jesus as an enlightened master would be on account of his preeminent status as an Elohim.

<hr/>

When Jesus Barsabbas, the Essene and enlightened master, was on Planet Earth some two thousand years ago, his message was not the message of Christianity today. The well-worn messages of Christianity are "The kingdom of God is nigh ..." and, of course, "the Lord God, Yahweh Elohim, is coming" at some time in the future, but we don't know precisely when. The churches want us to believe His arrival is imminent, and it might be, but the motivation of the churches is to plunder their membership for their own greedy ends. The same can be said of the statement that "Jesus is Lord." Well, of course he is, once the kingdom is established. But, two thousand years ago, whilst on Planet Earth, he was a man like any other. When the kingdom of God is established, Jesus will rightly return to what he was previously—for, possibly, billions of years—an Elohim, a god along with Michael, Gabriel, Lucifer, Raphael, and all the others (forgive me for not naming all the archangels and other beings).

As an Elohim, a god, we know that Jesus was to receive Planet Earth from Yahweh Elohim, the Lord God, as a reward for his work upon earth. However, whilst on Planet Earth, Jesus the Essene, living in Palestine was a man, and he died like any other man, possibly in Rome. He didn't die for us, or to pay the ultimate penalty for our sins and the sins of the world (particularly "original sin," another concoction of the Catholic Church, as was the story Adam and Eve in the Garden of Eden, munching on apples). He didn't ascend to heaven and become one member of the Holy Trinity, sitting on the right hand of God the Father (which would be most uncomfortable; kidding!).

During Jesus's time as an Elohim working with his friends on Planet Earth, he was a god, appointed to work on Planet Earth by Yahweh Elohim. However, when Jesus was on Planet Earth two thousand years ago, he was a man—albeit an extraordinary, extremely good, kind, loving, gentle man, but still a man. What made him an enlightened master was his inclusive message, not the pablum spouted by the so-called Christian churches mentioned above. Jesus's message is the same message I would give to you.

<hr>

As the biblical reference quoted below again and again and again clearly shows, Jesus's message was "Ye are gods.":

> Jesus answered them, "Is it not written in your law, 'I said, Ye are gods?' If he called them gods, unto whom the word of God came, and the scripture cannot be broken; Say ye of him whom the Father has sanctified and sent into the world, 'Thou blasphemest'; because I said, 'I am the Son of God'?"[19] [20]

He didn't just say, "You are the sons of God"; he didn't just say, "You are all children of God." Remember, those messages were well known and completely accepted by all Jews: Essenes, Pharisees, Sadducees, and Zealots alike. No, the Jews who wanted to stone Jesus to death, as recorded in John 10:34–36, had taken offence with Jesus because Jesus's message was "Ye are gods—and I am also god!" To the Essenes gathering up rocks to stone Jesus to death, the message "I am god: was blasphemy, a stoning offence.

I have made this point a few times in this story (in chapter

---

[19] Psalm 82:6: "I have said, Ye are gods and all of you are children of the most High."

[20] John 10:34–36.

8 and elsewhere). I have quoted the biblical passage, above, numerous times. You are probably sick of my repetition of it, and you can probably quote it word for word. But when we understand and accept who we truly are, we become enlightened.

<hr />

What is enlightenment? Osho's followers made a three-part opus entitled *The Book,* a compendium of his more memorable quotes. In series 1, from A to H, he devotes about thirteen pages, taken from four different books that discourse on the topic of enlightenment, to Gautama Siddhartha, the Buddha, who describes enlightenment with the words *anatta* and *nirvana.* Osho defines anatta this way: "*anatta* means no-self, no-soul, no-being. He not only denies the ego, he denies every possibility of the ego. Otherwise the ego is so cunning it will go on coming back again and again, it will find subtle ways to catch hold of you - it will come in the name of 'the Self', in fact it will come loudly in the name of the Self"[21]. Buddha's term nirvana is defined this way: "... a transcendent state in which there is neither suffering, desire, nor sense of self, and the subject is released from the effects of karma and the cycle of death and rebirth. It represents the final goal of Buddhism."[22] Osho would say that enlightenment is a state of nothingness, of being at one with the entire universe.

Buddha's way, Osho called the middle way: "The Path

<hr />

[21] *The Book: An Introduction to the Teachings of Bhagwan Shree Rajneesh,* series 1, from A to H (Rajneeshpuram, Oregon 97741, USA; Rajneesh Foundation International, 1984), 451.

[22] Wikipedia; Wikipedia's entry for the goal of Buddhism.

to Enlightenment is the Middle way. It is the Line Between all Opposite Extremes." Buddha, born Gautama Siddhartha, was a prince, the son of the king of the Indian state of Bihar, a small kingdom in northern India, bordering Nepal. He was married and had a newly born son. He abandoned everything to live an ascetic life of flagellating and starving the body, and meditating. He did this for several years, until, one day, he heard a man in a small boat instructing his son on how to tune a sitar, saying: "If you tighten the string too much it will break. And if you leave it too slack it will not play."

On hearing this, Buddha realised that he must follow the middle way, and he abandoned his asceticism. His fellow ascetics abandoned him for a time, but most eventually returned to him.

An Elohim, a god, in its noncorporeal state is universal, body-less, as both Osho and Gautama Buddha described. An Elohim can take on a corporeal form, as the Elohim Jesus did from time to time, as he and his friends re-created Planet Project Earth at the behest of Yahweh Elohim. But the man Jesus, the Essene living in Palestine over two thousand years ago, received the message from Yahweh Elohim—or some such source—that he was a god. He quoted the passage from Psalm 82:6 (later reiterated in John 10:34–36) stating that "Ye are gods." That became his message, his *gospel,* disseminated to his followers and to his fellow Essenes. That is one of the reasons why there was such opposition to him and why he was crucified.

The realisation of his true nature—that he had been an Elohim, one of the gods that created the world he was living in—was an enlightening moment for him, and me. He came to realise that we are all accompanied by a guardian Elohim, or angel, and have the nature of an Elohim residing within us. Every human on Planet Earth is so endowed. Eventually, perhaps after many lives and lessons upon Planet Earth, we become Elohim, in our perfected state: a universal spirit, no body, no self, no being, no ego; anatta, as Buddha would say. Buddha would contend that once that point is reached, we have attained nirvana—nothingness, enlightenment.

CHAPTER 10

GOD IN US: THE PRESENCE OF EVIL

I have written about Lucifer and his so-called rebellion against Yahweh Elohim, the Lord God. As I have previously written, Yahweh Elohim called Lucifer the Morning Star and the Shining One. I've arrived at an understanding, by means of this story, that Lucifer's problem was ego, which may be one of the potential products of free will.

However, I have read an account in Isaiah 14:13–15, where Lucifer is reported to have held the following notion:

> "But you said in your heart, 'I will ascend to heaven; I will raise my throne above the stars of God, And I will sit on the mount of assembly In the recesses of the north. I will ascend above the heights of the clouds; I will make myself like the Most High.' "Nevertheless you will be thrust down to Sheol, To the recesses of the pit. ..."

In keeping with my assertion that no one has ever heard

Yahweh Elohim or Lucifer or any of the Elohim speak, we find Isaiah able to read the mind of Lucifer, an arch-Elohim, and to interpret his thoughts in the quoted passage, above. Quite a feat of legilimancy, the capacity to read someone's thoughts. (I would perhaps exclude the Elohim Jesus and his companions from my assertion above, in regard to humans hearing the Elohim speak. When he and his crew on Project Planet Earth created men and women in their image, I expect that they [Jesus and his companions] appeared as men and women, and, as such, would probably have found it necessary to speak to the newly created humans. Those humans, in turn, would have heard the Elohim speak.)

All that said, I further expect that Isaiah allowed himself a little poetic licence when he wrote of Lucifer. The Judaic and Christian religions paint Lucifer as the fallen star, the great deceiver, Satan, the devil, and so on, and his companions as demons. I've said it before: these titles (Satan, the devil, and the like) are in keeping with the opinions of the religions of today. Like our national and political leaders, who need a foil, an adversary to continually oppose, so it is with religions and their leaders. An adversary like Lucifer keeps the members of our Christian churches focused on sin and the need for the redeeming act of the Lord Jesus to pay the penalty for human sins. Thus, church members are forced to live in a state of dependency upon the church and its clergy. Political and national leaders need an adversary to justify their hot and cold wars, and our participation in this or that war, which then leads to the need to produce materials of war. The financial expenditure and cost of which go to make the profits that line the pockets of the wealthy and the avaricious.

I've pointed out previously that I am not an apologist

for Lucifer, and I am not. I feel, however, that he has been maligned by religions past and present. If Yahweh Elohim trusted him enough to give him dominion over Planet Earth, until that dominion is transferred to the Elohim Jesus and his group, I don't see how we can disagree with Yahweh Elohim, the Lord God. However, His omniscience and omnipotence do not preclude the existence of evil in this world.

In fact, we all can recount stories of terrible evils in this world, committed at the orders of men like Adolf Hitler, Adolf Eichmann, Josef Stalin, Mao Tse-Tung, Idi Amin, Pol Pot, and countless other brutes coming down throughout history. There have been truly evil people—men and some women—who were the epitome of evil and who committed ghastly deeds, taking the lives of millions of men, women, and children, and even animals like whales, elephants, and many others.

I have heard it said that what tyrants fear most is the people they oppress, because they know that, one day, one of the oppressed will rise up and overthrow the tyranny. But that is not evil, per se; that is the normal expression of human nature. On a smaller scale, we see it in our political parties, when the leader is overthrown in a coup. The winner will have previously disavowed ever challenging for leadership and, instead, will claim that he or she was innocently carried to leadership by popular consensus, which the winner, in all honesty, could not refuse. This is the way human nature works. It's not evil, but it is shonky.

Evil does exist where psychopathic/sociopathic office managers can selectively terrorise some of their workers, whilst simultaneously encouraging a coterie of sycophants. Those terrorised can be terrorised because they are vulnerable and need their jobs to support their families. Psychopathy and sociopathy are evil, and they are very hard to spot, since the terrorised are too afraid to cry for help. The psychopathic/sociopathic manager or business leader is without a conscience and revels in his or her power. I know this to be true because I've seen it in my psychology practice.

I hold, and I expect many other psychologists would hold, that most human beings are not inherently evil. We may sin and do wrong, but we are not evil. Nevertheless, evil does exist, and it manifests in human behaviour, as described above. Moreover, a person does not have to massacre an entire village to be classified as evil, or to be seen as exhibiting evil actions or behaviour.

One of my patients—I will call her Sally (not her real name)—was frequently sexually abused by her father after he returned from South Vietnam. He even shared his daughter with some of his army friends. Sally's mother was continually drunk and couldn't protect her daughter. Sally raised a puppy under her bed, unbeknownst to her father. One night, she cried out during the rape, and the dog attacked her father. Her father murdered her dog and then gave Sally a shovel to use to bury her beloved friend. She attacked her father with the shovel and nearly cut off his fingers.

At the age of twelve, she ran away from home, lived on the streets of Sydney, and earned her living by selling her body. Eventually, she got her life into order and studied a trade, which became her life's work.

Another patient, Roger (not his real name), was six or seven years old when he and his older brothers and sisters were sold by their parents to men, for fifty-dollars a time. This practice went on for many years, until the mother threw her husband out of the home. She then took Roger into her bed until he was about fifteen years of age.

Fortunately, I do not have a lot of stories like these, but I do have others. I became physically ill when my patients told me these stories. From the two examples shared, you get the gist of some of the evil that families can perpetrate against their children. Naturally, these are not atrocities of the scope of murdering of six million Jews, largely on the orders of the Nazi Colonel Adolf Eichmann during Hitler's regime in World War. I expect that Eichmann, far removed from the gas chambers and ovens of Auschwitz and the other concentration camps, would not have felt responsible—or, at least, no more responsible than the German guards at the camps.

Although it is not of the enormity of genocide, there is great evil in some Australian families, with the father committing domestic violence against the mother, beating and raping the children, and even murdering the mother and children. A lady once told me that her husband, when they were newly married—in fact, on the day of their wedding—said to her, "If you ever play up on me, it will be a bullet in the head for you." She has never played up and is still alive … I hope.

What does the foregoing have to do with the God in us, and our relationship with the Elohim assigned to us?

I have proposed that each human on Planet Earth has at least two Elohim in attendance—a guardian Elohim (or guardian angel, as some prefer to call such spirit beings) and, perhaps, an attending/accompanying Elohim as well, whose purpose is to experience human life through the human to whom they are assigned and thereby have their own natures changes by that experience. Are the Elohim with each human being the ones responsible for the evil perpetrated by that human? Or is it human nature manifested through the human life force that is ultimately responsible for atrocities?

Elohim, who are immortal and therefore experiencing "everlasting life," would have a lot to lose if they were responsible for the direct and, perhaps, even the indirect taking of life. The Elohim were created by Yahweh Elohim, and whilst character flaws may have developed in them through the application of free will, it seems unlikely that the Elohim would risk losing their immortality and everlasting life. That would be a lot to lose. Still, they might be willing to risk it; nothing is impossible.

All that said, it therefore seems to me that it is human nature, through the human life force, that is largely responsible for the atrocities on our planet. It is my considered opinion that the evil in our societies is the result of human nature—and that evil runs the gamut from ritual murder, or so-called honour killing, of wives in India and some Middle Eastern countries by family members for "shaming" the family, to the sexual, physical, emotional, and psychological abuse of wives and children.

But, whilst the perpetrators of evil in our society seem to be unaffected by their own cruelty—until brought to some form of justice and forced to make recompense for their crimes—what of the Elohim that accompany them? I expect that they are sorely affected and afflicted.

Imagine having to live through the experiences of an ogre like Adolf Eichmann, who, with the stroke of a pen, sent millions of Jews to the gas chambers and ovens. Eichmann, residing in a South American country after the war, was eventually apprehended by the Israeli Mossad and brought to Israel to stand trial for his crimes and evil acts.

Do Eichmann's sins, though recorded in history books for posterity, evaporate upon the death of the human body and the conversion of the human life force to a form of universal energy? Or, does the evil of Adolf Eichmann continue to exist as universal energy in some converted form, particularly if energy can neither be created nor destroyed?

These are very deep questions to ponder. When the Bible says, "The spirit returns to the God that gave it," I consider it is referring to the Elohim that accompanied the human being while he or she was alive: the guardian Elohim and the attending/accompanying Elohim. This passage suggests that the spirit of an Elohim departs when the host, or human body, dies and the human life force leaves the body. The human body is then merely an empty shell, and the spirit of the Elohim returns to Yahweh Elohim, the Lord God, and awaits, if required, to return to Planet Earth to be with another human being. But what if an imprint of the energy or soul of the human life force remains intact? In other words, is there some sort of repository of the energy of the human life force?

Christianity appears to believe this is so. It seems to me that this assertion is the whole basis for heaven, hell, limbo, purgatory, and the like. But, if the above passage is talking about the eternal spirit of the Elohim returning to Yahweh Elohim, where does that leave the Christian doctrines of heaven, hell, and so on?

If there is an energy imprint of the human life force housed in some sort of repository somewhere in this universe, then there is also the energy of a hellish amount of sin, evil, and atrocity all in one place. Perhaps that is one of the reasons, for the black holes and desculators created by the seven Ones in the seven universes. I can imagine some sort of immense compactor to crush all that sin and evil to almost nothingness and then transmute that gargantuan amount of energy into garden mulch for growing orchids in Universe Three, the garden universe. Quite a bit of foresight on the part of the Ones!

Such a compactor would do away with the need for hell, limbo, and purgatory. I do not feel that any of the Ones is a brutal fiend who revels in the idea of energy imprints crackling and burning in the fires of hell for all eternity. And what of the crimes of the man who drank too much, got arrested for urinating in the gutter of the main street, and then died in the police booze-tank on a Sunday, without attending Mass and therefore in a state of unconfessed mortal sin? Was he to receive the punishment of eternally crackling and burning in hell, when his sins were compared with the evil deeds and atrocities of an ogre like Adolf Eichmann?

CHAPTER 11

GOD IN US: WHEN GOD
BECOMES WANTON

When Yahweh Elohim ceded dominion of Planet Earth to Lucifer for a thousand years, the Randy 96K followed Lucifer and his administrative team to Planet Earth. Their intent was to have their way with the human men and women on earth and then return to the heavens. However, when their sexual lust was sated, they tried to return to Yahweh Elohim's heavenly realm, only to find their return barred by the Archangel Michael. What did they do? (Two possible options were discussed earlier, in chapter 3.)

Not all the Randy 96K returned to Yahweh Elohim's presence when they were finally allowed to return by Michael. I say this knowing the penchant of free will, in both Elohim and humans, to do what it likes and pleases; it would therefore seem likely that a sizable proportion of Elohim remained on Planet Earth of their own volition.

To be one unranked Elohim among 240,000 others was not particularly distinguished. But to be a god to millions of human beings, both men and women, would be most titillating and ego enhancing. There would be side benefits.

Not only would there be the adulation of millions, there would also sexual benefits, as well as huge financial rewards. In short, one could live like a god. Imagine being a god to millions instead of a work-horse on some distant nebula or far-flung galaxy, toiling for various archangels under Yahweh Elohim. The latter might not be very enticing in the minds of some.

The majority of the Randy 96K were undoubtedly sensible spirit beings who, in the heat of the moment, probably made a mistake in coming to Planet Earth for the reasons they did. Some few, undoubtedly, would have been self-serving types whose only loyalty was to themselves and their own wanton desires. Combine such beings with truly evil humans, like the future Gestapo leader, Heimlich Himmler, and you have a recipe for great evil in the world. As you will recall, the only stipulation for the Elohim themselves was that they could not intentionally destroy or take the lives of humans and animals; if they did so, their eternal life would be forfeited, and they would eventually die just like humans. But such a limitation as the taking of life, if they saw it as a limitation, was easily circumvented by any number of willing, conscienceless, psychopathic humans.

To such Elohim, appearances were important. To be viewed as a king with godlike powers was very rewarding and ego enhancing, but to be beautiful, to never age, and to be worshipped as a god—not merely as one who is godlike—was the ideal. To live in palatial mansions, to be heaped with riches beyond their imagination, to have their every need met, and to be served by willing, obsequious servants who paid them all due respect, was also ideal. Such Elohim saw all this as their due.

And, Yahweh Elohim and Lucifer watched. ...

———————◆◇◇◆———————

Today, we see the foregoing in the trappings of some of the richest and most powerful families on Planet Earth. There were, however, limitations. Some 200,000 years ago, when *Homo sapiens* first appeared on Planet Earth, created by the Elohim Jesus and his band of willing workers, human needs were very basic. Food was either hunted or caught; the growing of crops was very rudimentary and, naturally, ruled by the seasons. For the Elohim, sexual pleasures with human beings might have been abundant, but riches, pleasures, and ease were many thousands of years away—perhaps 150,000 years away, or even more.

Eventually, however, human kingdoms were established. Kings were crowned, and royal families, assisted by the Elohim, were founded all around the globe. It became apparent very early in the history of humankind that being the power in the background, perhaps behind the throne, and having a level of anonymity was much more fulfilling than the ego-enhancing glories of recognition and worship by the hordes of unwashed savage subjects with their constant clamouring for audiences and favours. Early in human history, even the newly founded royalty was largely unwashed, and their palaces were little better than stables—in fact, they often *were* stables where they slept with their horses. Remote kingdoms in outer China and Mongolia were mighty and very warlike but the living quarters were yurts, devilishly cold in winter and smelly beyond imagination. There was not a centrally heated palace to be found in thousands of leagues.

The region of Mesopotamia, on the other hand, was

becoming somewhat pleasurable, and the city of Babylon, on the Euphrates River, was becoming a place of residence worthy of a god, with its royal palace that would eventually to showcase the Hanging Gardens of Babylon, built by King Nebuchadnezzar II for his wife. Babylon did not quite match the splendours of Yahweh Elohim's heavenly realm, but it was on the way to becoming a fitting place for lowly, unranked Elohim to reside, where they could be recognised and treated as gods.

We do not know the exact number of the Randy 96K who remained on Planet Earth after they were given permission to return to the heavenly realm and back into the service of Yahweh Elohim. There might be a little more than 2,000 billionaires, excluding royalty and dictators, in the world today, with a net worth of some 7.7 trillion dollars[23]. But the Elohim on Planet Earth were hidden and secretive and would never appear on the Forbes list of the richest people. It becomes hard to explain how a person, male or female, can look astoundingly beautiful and never appear to age. So, it might be an estimate, once again, that something less than one or two in a thousand, or ninety-six individuals—or, at the most, less than two hundred individual Elohim—remained on Planet Earth to live like kings and gods. But all were—and still are—watched by Yahweh Elohim, the archangels Michael and Lucifer, and all the unranked Elohim ... including Jesus.

---

[23] Wikipedia; Wikipedia's entry for Billionaires.

That the Elohim remaining on Planet Earth have become rich beyond all the dreams of avarice is undisputable. If two of the richest people in the *Forbes* list are worth many billions of dollars each, and whilst still living, made all that wealth in just one lifetime, how might the remaining Elohim fare in 2,857 seventy-year lifetimes over the 200,000 years of the history of *Homo sapiens* on Planet Earth? Even if they accrued their riches over a paltry 50,000 years, or 714 seventy-year lifetimes, they would still be rich beyond all dreams of avarice. Okay, accrual of wealth would be slower at the start of the 50,000 years, but it would still accrue exponentially over the entire period.

We must remember here that we are dealing with gods—indestructible, never aging, never dying, with powers that calmed the savage seas of Planet Earth, that raised dry land and filled it with vegetation after first dissipating the intense cloud cover shrouding the earth so that the sun could shine and allow plants to grow. Remember, the Elohim stocked the oceans with all manner of marine creatures, filled the land with animals, and then created men and women in their own image (well, at least the Elohim Jesus and his trusty crew did all those things). With the remaining Elohim of the Randy 96K, we are talking about powerful spirit beings living on Planet Earth, whom Yahweh Elohim used to help Him subdue the Milky Way galaxy. Couldn't those powerful spirit beings create gold, diamonds, and all sorts of treasures in just one lifetime?

In addition to the creation, manufacture, and accrual of indescribable amounts of wealth, we have the assumption of power—proxy power, perhaps, but power nonetheless—that they could wield through a multitude of willing thugs. Some few of the willing psychopathic thugs would, astoundingly enough, have brains and could become owners and/or managers of the businesses funded and factored by the Elohim and their banking and investment interests. These men and women became the families of the upper, noble, and ruling classes of the countries where the various Elohim made their homes.

From this point forward, we shall use the group corporate name that they, the Elohim, themselves assumed: the Daemon Corporation. Acquiring huge tracts of land ceded to them by the ruling classes, the Daemon Corporation members started building their mansions.

Fifty thousand years ago, competition was scarce, and humans were only just coming out of the Stone Age, just beginning to forge copper and bronze for their swords and arrowheads. Thus, members of the Daemon Corporation had another significant advantage in that they, like the seven Ones of all seven universes, had learned how to *mind link* with one another, around the entire globe, and thereby know one another's thoughts without the need for physical proximity. Thus, from the earliest of times, the Daemon Corporation was a financial investment and manufacturing conglomerate that circled much of the globe, connecting all the major cities and commercial centres.

The Daemons—which they used as their family name, for, indeed, they saw themselves as a family—initially used Babylon as their meeting place for the Daemon Corporation's thirteen-member board of directors. Whilst the mind link allowed them the ability to effortlessly communicate over immense distances, they also had the ability to teleport themselves to anywhere on the globe in fractions of seconds;

they called it *apportation* and *disapportation* (or, *apporting*, for short.) This ability to apport should not be seen as unusual. How else could all the Ones' of the seven universes move from galaxy to galaxy? The desculator system via wormholes connected universes to one another. The system was designed for inter- and intra-galaxy travel; it took too long to walk, and humans wouldn't invent spaceships for more than another 49,950 years.

There were (and are) few human abilities that could compare with the abilities of the Daemons. What the Daemons lacked, however, and what some humans had in abundance, was their sense of innovation. Why develop vehicles that flew or could be driven along the ground when you could apport yourself wherever you wanted to go? The Daemons never considered for one moment the need to invent anything that they had the ability to perform themselves. Whilst initially travel on Planet Earth was either by foot, horse, or camel—or, more rarely, elephant—eventually, humans crafted horse-drawn carts that could carry heavy loads and groups of people and soldiers. In time, automobiles were invented, along with aircraft designed to carry hundreds of passengers in comfort. Again, these all were the inventions of innovative humans; the Daemons had no reason to even consider inventing such things. Thus, humans invented large buses to transport groups of humans; they invented B-Double freightliners to carry goods, and ships to cross the seas. So, Planet Earth, as an investment opportunity, was all sewn up, and the Daemon Corporation was quick to finance and support human efforts to make up their innovative shortfall.

The problem with many humans is that they are warlike, and that this capacity exists along with the free will they possess, just like the Elohim. The Elohim—the Daemons—could not be warlike. The Daemons' might have the capacity to slay whole armies with just a word or a look, but they were forbidden to do so. Humans with free will were not so forbidden.

It has been said that "war is just theft writ large." The Daemon Corporation was ideally placed to take advantage of humans' warlike nature to maximise land holdings and profits. Wars and the production of war materials was a great source of profit. The Daemon Corporation financed and backed just about every war on Planet Earth. It will be a sad day for some when Jesus returns to Planet Earth, as wars will be outlawed, and peace will reign supreme.

In the meantime, Yahweh Elohim, the archangels Michael and Lucifer, and all the unranked Elohim—including Jesus—all continue to watch. …

CHAPTER 12

GOD IN US: LUCIFER'S TALE

Background Provided by the Archangel Lucifer

When I opened my eyes for the very first time, I was lying, fully grown, on some sort of bower, surrounded by sweet-smelling blooms in the presence of an indescribable soft, warm, golden light. I immediately prostrated myself in the presence of Yahweh Elohim, or the Lord, as I call him. I was alive and in the presence of the Lord God, our One of our universe, and I rejoiced that the Lord had given me such honour as to have created me and given me life.

The Lord had fashioned me a physical body that could be transmuted into spirit at will, and the Lord was experimenting with a tangible physical body for Himself. I was one of the first among many brethren. Soon, I was joined by Gabriel and Michael who was the first created. I have always been close with both. Whilst none of us had any sense of what we would eventually recognise as *time*, in time Gabriel, Michael, and I were joined by other arch-Elohim—or *archangels*, as we would eventually be called. Also, in time, we would be joined by many thousands of other Elohim.

The Lord had named me Lucifer—the Morning Star, the Shining One. I was the one of the first He created, and one of the first He named, but he named each Elohim in turn. He initially created 240,000 Elohim, and it was our duty and pleasure to assist Him in forming and creating our universe.

Originally, before any universe existed at all, there were seven spirits—gods—born of the same source, and that source was unknown and unknowable. The seven Lord Gods called themselves "the Ones," and each One set about harnessing the product of the singularity that resulted from the Big Bang that started the entire process. The singularity from nothing, nothing at all, made the "stuff" of which each universe was made: gases, chemicals, and space dust that coalesced into galaxies, solar systems, and planets.

Initially, our job, the Elohim's work, was the big picture: to help form the billions of galaxies that, on a large scale, filled our universe. My job was to oversee the creation of the Milky Way galaxy, the Andromeda galaxy, the Elliptical galaxy, and hundreds of other galaxies. I was busy, and whilst I was new to the idea of emotions, I recognised that I loved it.

Planet Earth was created as a by-product of our singularity, and it became a special project called Project Planet Earth. A particularly enthusiastic, creative, gifted Elohim named Jesus, was given the honour of leading Project Planet Earth, which would culminate in the first human being to ever inhabit a planet in our universe—or any of the seven universes, for that matter. This was a well-disguised secret of our One. I don't think He wanted to pre-empt the event of the creation of humans.

You might ask, Why the secrecy? It wasn't a competition between the Ones; rather, it was because humans, made in the image of the gods, the Elohim themselves, appeared to be so like us. There had been false starts in the creation of the first humans, and the Lord did not want to raise our hopes, in case the creation process didn't work as expected. We may be gods, but, unlike the Lord, we make mistakes.

I helped Jesus as time permitted. We all had a very clear sense of time, now that the distances between galaxies and solar systems had become known and recognised. I was helping to create hundreds of galaxies and solar systems that were initially empty. I would have helped Jesus more frequently, but duty called in hundreds of other places. Still, the ever-inventive Jesus and his hundred-strong crew of Elohim worked tirelessly to fulfil the Lord's wishes for a planet inhabited by beautiful vegetation (supplied by another universe), sea creatures (also supplied by another universe), suitable animals (supplied by yet another universe), after our disastrous false start with the dinosaurs. The Lord wanted human beings to inhabit Planet Earth, and Jesus and his friends created humans in their own image. Male and female humans, alike, all were created by the Elohim of Jesus's crew.

The Lord was amazed that the lowly Elohim Jesus and his crew of willing workers had completed Project Planet Earth in record time. They had created the first human-inhabited planet in any of the seven universes. Our One was overjoyed by the work of Jesus and decided to give Planet Earth as a gift to Jesus and his crew.

Whilst I hadn't worked as frequently as I would have liked with Jesus, I had helped him. The Lord's determination to give Jesus Planet Earth as a gift caught me off balance. I felt hurt that the Lord had not recognised my tireless work in hundreds of galaxies. I complained to the Lord, for the first time in my life, because I felt unloved—or, at least, less loved—and somehow diminished by the Lord's intention. However, as we all know, the Lord changed His mind and ceded Planet Earth to me for a thousand years. Jesus took the Lord's change of intention in his stride, as did his crew. My temper tantrum neither angered nor annoyed Jesus.

That thousand years was really an indeterminant period, but I assembled my crew, who were my friends, and we took up residence on Planet Earth. In addition to my friends who would help me administer Planet Earth, we were soon joined by a large band of Elohim. Some have said it was one-third of the heavenly host, or about 96,000 Elohim. Someone else called them the Randy 96K, because it was their intention to have sex with the human beings that Jesus and his crew had created. Whilst I was nominally in charge of Planet Earth, I didn't feel it incumbent upon me or my friends to get mixed up in their sordid activities. Apparently, though, the Lord was not impressed either, and He set the Archangel Michael the task of preventing the horde from returning and re-entering His heavenly domain.

So, my team and I had some 96,000 unexpected guests. By that time, I had taken up residence and, as happenstance would have it, built my permanent home beside the Tiber River on the bend of the river that would eventually be situated opposite Vatican City (the construction of the Vatican was many, many thousands of years into the future, of course). It was beautiful spot, and my partner, Esther, accompanied me there. I sent more than 150 of my team to all regions where humans lived on Planet Earth. Their job was to help and civilise the humans.

It is interesting to realise that the physical diversity of the humans created by the Elohim mirrored the diversity of the Elohim who created them. This made the assigning of work to my Elohim simpler, because we could send Elohim with the appearance of the Chinese to China, or Elohim with the appears of the Japanese person to the islands of Japan, and the like. This made my Elohim less conspicuous, and the work of bringing the humans out of their very savage and backward state into a form of civilisation became much easier and more rewarding. We taught them language, basic work and food-cultivation skills, and so forth—all of which they would need to live in harmony together. These things were also very new to us.

Interview of the Archangel Lucifer by the Elohim Lisa, John, and Jesus

It was hoped that an interview with Archangel Lucifer would answer the many questions that have become apparent in human history. Lisa is the human John's guardian Elohim, and the Elohim John accompanies the human John and experiences his life. Jesus needs no introduction. The interview was conducted via mind link with the presence of Lucifer, in his home on the banks of the Tiber River opposite the Vatican City in Rome, Italy, in the year 2018. The contents of the mind link session were then relayed to the human John, who could not be physically present.

Lisa: Considering that I'm the little girlie here among all you macho males, perhaps I should start the ball rolling and ask Lucifer the first question.

Lucifer: I remember you, Lisa, from Alpha Centauri. You were cheeky there too.

Lisa: (Chuckles.) I remember you too. I'd like to know how long you have been on Planet Earth.

Lucifer: I was sent here to Planet Earth by the Lord nearly 200,000 years ago, soon after Jesus created the species *Homo sapiens.* I had visited previously and watched the unsuccessful attempts at creating the species of humans that became known as *Pithecanthropus erectus,* Java man, *Homo erectus,* and, later, Neanderthal, a sub-species of *Homo sapiens.*

Jesus was very inventive.

When Jesus was away touring the universe with the Lord, in his absence, his crew tried to create animals but only succeeded in creating dinosaurs—Tyrannosaurus rex and the like—completely unsuited to living alongside humans. Fortunately, that experiment died out, and we sourced suitable animals from the universe that created animals.

Jesus: There has been a lot of controversy among humans, particularly the members of religions—Judaism and Christianity mostly—with your coming to Planet Earth. Earth will become my gift from Yahweh Elohim someday, but you are cast as the archdemon, Satan, the Adversary opposing Yahweh Elohim's actions and intentions. What are your feelings on these matters?

Lucifer: I will admit that the Lord's action in planning to give you Planet Earth was a shock. Strangely, I felt hurt and rejected by the Lord. These were new emotions for me. I had never experienced them before, and I did not know how to deal with those strange and painful feelings.

I return to the Lord's heavenly domain whenever I like; there is no problem, and I am not banned or barred from His presence. I report to the Lord frequently, telling Him of the progress being made here, and we have had many long discussions.

I told Him that his action in gifting Planet Earth to you felt like He was rejecting me, and I felt hurt. He told me that He did it on purpose. He hadn't cleared it with you first. You didn't know about it and were completely surprised, but you took His turnabout completely in your stride and were not hurt by the loss of Planet Earth, at the time, at all. He said that He wanted to teach everyone a lesson, and I was the one He chose as the guinea pig, so to speak. He told me that He didn't want or intend to hurt me, but He said He knew that I could take the apparent snub and rejection in my stride which, as it turned out, I didn't. That surprised the Lord.

When I first came down to Planet Earth I was still hurt. I realised, however, that it was my pride that was hurt—it was my ego running amok and getting the better of me. I immediately returned to the Lord's heavenly domain and apologised to Him. I also thought on the matter for a few thousand years, and I realised just how much my ego had felt damaged. I suppose it was that He chose you, and not me for the reward and for the distinction that Planet Earth was the first planet inhabited by humans. There are thousands of planets now, and humans are in every one of the seven universes—humans created by you, Jesus. Nevertheless, the rejection hurt my ego, and when I eventually realised what had motivated me, I returned to the Lord's heavenly domain, prostrated myself in humble supplication, and apologised. He responded by congratulating me on providing an excellent lesson in ego management for everyone to see. I suppose I was a little less sanguine about it than He.

John: There is a scripture written by Isaiah—I think it's Isaiah 14:13–15—where you were reported to have said in your heart:

> "I will ascend to heaven; I will raise my throne above the stars of God, And I will sit on the mount of assembly In the recesses of the north. I will ascend above the heights of the clouds; I will make myself like the Most High."

Did you say that in your heart?

Lucifer: The short answer is no. I never said that in my heart or my head or aloud or in any way. How Isaiah could know what was going on in my mind remains a mystery to me. I am an archangel, which is pretty high up in the scheme of things in this universe. But I do not care about being the biggest and the best among the Elohim; I never really wanted that distinction anyway. The Lord is my Lord and creator, and I will do my best, but I have no interest in being "like the Most High." This universe has one Most High. It isn't me, and it never will be me; but it *is* and *always will be* the Lord.

I think you need to remember that being a prophet of god among the ancient followers of Judaism was a major social and religious distinction. It counted within Jewish society. To claim that I was or am this *bogeyman* who opposes the Lord is still a very popular myth among the leaders of the Jewish and Christian religions even today, for that matter. They always have someone to blame.

I think I need to get a new press secretary; doing my own public relations isn't working very well.

Does all that answer your question? Are you satisfied with my answer?

John: Yes, it does satisfy me, but, the earth is full of claims that you are Satan—the devil, the Adversary—and that you are opposed to Judaism and Christianity and everything that is supposedly good on Planet Earth.

Lucifer: Who is making those claims? Do you know?

John: Well, I suppose it's Judaism and Christianity, and probably a few other religions on Planet Earth as well.

Lucifer: Yes, that's correct. The people that run those religions would have a lot to lose if it could be shown that I, supposedly the *bogeyman,* am not the *bogeyman* at all. By that, I mean that I am not really opposed to the Lord.

The ordinary people in the street do not really know or care about whether I exist. Mostly, they really don't believe I exist. They think that earth is like hell sometimes and that they must live through hell daily. I do the grocery shopping sometimes, not that I must eat anything, but just to judge the mood of the ordinary people in the marketplaces. They aren't interested in all this religious stuff at all. But the religions and the priests and ministers are ready to blame me for all the wars on this planet, and I have not started, encouraged, or participated in one single war on this planet in my nearly 200,000 years here—and I never will.

Lisa: I have been told that there are Elohim on this planet today who do foment wars. Is that true?

Lucifer: Yes, it is true. None of the perpetrators work in my crew, however. They started an organisation called the Daemon Corporation—as in *demon*—and their aim is the accrual of wealth and power for themselves on Planet Earth. Their aims and goals are very limited, superficial, and shallow. Originally, they came to Planet Earth as part of the Randy 96K and decided to stay. They aren't my people, but the Lord and I watch them closely, as does Jesus, I believe.

Jesus: Correct. One day I will have stewardship, together with my people, over this Planet Earth. Peace will reign, and the Daemon people will have to seek a new line of work.

Lucifer: I trust that that day will come soon. I will continue to live here, with your permission and as the Lord wills, but with all the appearances of an ordinary citizen. Never having to eat or sleep gives a wise person considerable available time and the ability to study all manner of things. I read, speak, and translate Hebrew, Attic Greek, Aramaic, and a host of other languages. I have qualifications as a doctor of medicine, a research scientist, an astronomer, and many more. I could use these qualifications anywhere, but I like it down here. It's been my home now for nearly 200,000 years.

I can't wait to hand the administrative and spiritual reins over to Jesus.

Lisa: Why haven't you tried to stop these Daemon people, or at least stamp them out—send them packing back to the heavens?

Lucifer: I wanted to get rid of them from Planet Earth, and I spoke to the Lord about it, but He asked me to not become involved. They employ and use many humans, and a confrontation with us that might cause the loss of human life must be avoided, even though the Daemons' henchmen are responsible for the deaths of millions of humans. If we killed one human, it would be a tragedy, I feel. I think He has other lessons to teach us with this situation. I just do what He tells me. "I'm a lover not a fighter," as the saying goes.

John: In the Garden of Eden, you are pictured as a snake that tempted Eve to eat the fruit of the Tree of the Knowledge of Good and Evil. Were you ever a snake, and did that actually happen? What do you think of the Christian doctrine of original sin?

Lucifer: Do I look long and thin to you? No, I've never been a snake—in the Garden of Eden, or anywhere else, for that matter. The devil is the one that's portrayed as the spirit being that tempted Eve. It wasn't me acting the part of the devil, or a demon. I wasn't there. This is an ancient story, one of the many myths passed on to humans through oral tradition. The only gods on Planet Earth when Eve was a slip of a girl, so to speak, were Jesus's crew. Did you or any of your people ever try to tempt Eve, Jesus?

Jesus: No. There was never an Eve, or an Adam, for that matter. There was no Garden of Eden. There was no apple orchard, and Eve never ate of the fruit. There was no Tree of the Knowledge of Good and Evil.

The story is told that the serpent deceived Eve and told her that she would not surely die if she ate of the fruit of the tree and would become "as a god" herself. This is a story concocted by Judaism—the Jewish religion—and by Christianity. No Elohim, and certainly not Yahweh Elohim, would ever use such tactics to coerce humans to commit such errors and to disobey their god. The whole exercise is completely pointless. It's the product of a very vivid and fertile Jewish imagination, and organised Christianity has willingly carried on the tradition.

Adam and Eve's supposed sin in eating of the fruit fostered the Christian doctrine of original sin. Humans, supposedly, must pay a penalty for the imaginary original sin of Adam and Eve. According to the doctrine, humans are all born in sin as a direct result of Adam and Eve's sin in disobeying god. Innocent babies who die before they are baptised are supposed to have the stain of original sin on their souls, and they must spend time in limbo (or *limbus infantium* or *limbus puerorum*)[24] to remove that stain of sin. What's fair and just about that? Nothing. It's a myth—a "pious myth," some have called such things, but still a myth. It is untrue, and the Lord

---

[24] Wikipedia; Wikipedia's entry for *Limbus Infantium* or *Limbus Puerorum.*

God has better things to do than to create mythical sins to trip up humans.

Another point to consider is the motive for such a concocted story. The Christian church promulgated the doctrine of original sin to, in effect, make ordinary church members dependent upon the church. They use other words to describe their actions, but dependency upon the church was the intent. (It still is, by the way.) The idea was to convince members of the Christian congregations that they were born in sin, and if they died in a state of serious, or mortal, sin, then they would crackle and burn forever in the eternal fires of hell, or Hades—which doesn't exist either. If you can get church members to believe that idea, you keep people dependent upon the church, the priests and ministers, for their spiritual well-being. That is not how the Elohim work, but this sort of thing is the way of some humans—not all, but some do work that way.

A final point to consider here is the age of these myths. My crew and I first created *Homo sapiens* some 200,000 years ago. That's the time that many of those stories describe. But writing wasn't invented until, maybe, 5,300 years ago. So, the stories were passed down orally through the generations, some 194,700 years or more. So, about 5,300 years ago, someone's fertile imagination created these stories that were supposed to have happened 194,700 years before, and he or she started writing them down. Once they were written down, they became divine writ.

Lisa: Oh! Very funny.

Jesus: Thank you. But oral traditions do not span

that number of years; people forget. Most people cannot remember what they had for breakfast this day a year ago, or even if they ate breakfast at all. So, how are they going to remember stories and myths that were created 5,300 years ago, let alone 194,700 years before that?

I realise that some African, Egyptian, and Middle Eastern tribes have individuals called "storytellers"— similar to present-day raconteurs, who are purposely trained to remember stories and genealogies by heart. It's often called "oral tradition," and it is very impressive to observe an individual recount complicated genealogies, histories, laws, and occurrences without making an error, telling such stories as the origins of all life or the Flood of Noah, or stories about their tribe meeting or observing beings who could not be anything but supernatural. They might be telling stories about my crew and me when we first made men and women and worked to civilise those tribes of people.

Those stories can vary in age but can be almost 200,000 years old, and they are quite accurately memorised. However, they often do not account for the hermeneutics extant at the time; often, they also do not have all the relevant information. Those stories are the basis of the myths recounted in the Bible.

Lucifer: Another point to consider, is the fact that the Lord intended to give Planet Earth to Jesus and his friends some five thousand years after the species of human that scientists now call *Homo sapiens* was created. Time means nothing to Yahweh Elohim, so by the time He changed His mind and ceded Planet Earth to me, there were about one million living human beings created in the image of Jesus and his friends. These were the humans that the so-called Randy 96K came down to Planet Earth to visit.

Initially, Jesus and his friends reported that they created three or four humans each, which means about four hundred humans were created in the image of the crew of Elohim. These humans were long-lived, surviving for hundreds of years, as compared to today's shorter life expectancies. For example, Noah and his family were each reputed to live some six to eight hundred years. A famous case recorded in the Bible was Methuselah, who lived for 969 years. It's quite feasible that there were at least one million or more humans on Planet Earth, spreading slowly around the globe, by the time I was given dominion over the earth.

(Pauses.) You might wonder what duties were given to me by the Lord. I came down to earth with 200 friends to help me; I kept 50 Elohim with me and sent the remaining 150 friends to all points of the compass where humans had migrated and were residing. The work I assigned to each Elohim was to help the humans to develop language and various civilising skills. The humans were initially hunter-gatherers. They made spears and learned from us how to make sparks and fire by striking flints together. We taught them how to fish and how to create fishing lines, bone hooks, nets, and traps. You must remember that all this was very new to us too. We have no need to eat or sleep, so the creation of weapons and traps was very new. The teaching of how to domesticate certain animals, such as cattle, sheep, and goats, also became important, providing sustainable food in the form of milk and some meat. Eventually, over thousands of years, we taught the humans how to cultivate various grains and vegetables. These were initially provided to us from the universe that creates them. The growing of vegetable and grain crops was a much more sedentary lifestyle than that of purely hunter-gathers. So, also, as a by-product, rudimentary towns and cities were built—these were the first trappings of civilisation.

You need to realise that the Elohim I sent around the globe could move easily and quickly by means of apportation. Can you imagine the confusion and wonder my Elohim caused having apported into the midst of a group of dour humans, who wore nothing but animal skins, whilst my Elohim dressed in sumptuous, colourful robes? Is it any wonder that such dour humans saw my friends as gods, bowing down to worship them as gods? Over many, many thousands of years, it is not difficult to conceive how these early humans created legends and myths about what their god did for them. This is how the myths around the Jewish patriarchs Abraham, Isaac, and Jacob were created. You need to remember too that the Elohim are assigned to humans as their guardian Elohim or angels and companions, as are Lisa and John here—invisible to humans but still present. Guardian Elohim are also assigned to countries, kingdoms, and governments.

I kept some fifty Elohim with me for administrative and staff-rotation purposes. Two Elohim, Isaac and Rebecca, have been my main helpers and support, though we shared the work with all fifty of us quite equitably. We all take turns working with the various tribes of humans. You should remember that the early humans may have been relatively long-lived, but none lived as long as my immortal Elohim lived. So, there were Elohim working with new humans every few hundred years. It was also very good experience for us and helped us understand the humans we worked with. There were very many truly lovely people among the tribes of humans with whom we worked, but there were some savage, power-hungry thugs who wanted to rule everyone else. They were very competitive and in league with the Daemon Corporation that helped to create royalty, kings, kingdoms, and nobility, as well as the military. We would never have fostered or approved of the creation of royalty, nobility, kings, and kingdoms, but the Lord wanted us to allow the humans the free will to work out their social and domestic affairs themselves. If we became involved and inadvertently killed a human, it would be disastrous for us.

(Pauses.) May we finish this interview with two topics of interest to me? That is not to say, of course, that all the subjects addressed were not highly interesting. The subjects are the so-called miracles of Jesus, and the return (or Second Coming) of Jesus Christ to Planet Earth, as prophesied in the book of Revelation and elsewhere. Do we agree? Good.

The Christian church, by means of various New Testament texts, stakes its claim to divinity through Jesus's miraculous birth: the indefinite conniption—oops … I mean, *immaculate conception*—the numerous miracles of Jesus, his resurrection from the dead after being crucified, and his ascension to heaven to sit at the right hand of God the Father. I ask him to comment upon these things.

Jesus: Firstly, I was the human man Jesus described in the New Testament of the Bible. I lived as a human on Planet Earth more than two thousand years ago, in Palestine, and I was born into the Barsabbas family, which belonged to the Essene sect of Judaism. My last human life, lived two thousand years ago, was the last of numerous human lives that I have lived on Planet Earth. I still come back to Planet Earth frequently as an Elohim spirit to visit Lucifer and Esther, and my other Elohim friends here. I still have a home here in Rome that I return to frequently and live in. Rome is very convenient for many reasons, and the Lord God has promised Planet Earth to be ceded to me as a gift from Him. That time is soon to come, though it has not yet been decided when that will happen.

A prophecy was supposedly made by the Archangel Gabriel that my mother, Mary, would bear a child conceived by miraculous means through the Holy Spirit, and that Elizabeth, the wife of the celibate Essene ascetic monk Zacharias, would also bear a child.

However, your friend and mine, Gabriel, did not make those prophecies, although they are attributed to him. The prophecies were made by an Essene Levite priest who assumed the mantle, or identity, of the Archangel Gabriel. This was not uncommon among the Essenes. Often, in the performance of priestly duties, the high priest, for example, might take on the identity of an Elohim, or even Yahweh Elohim. In this case, a priest took on Gabriel's identity in order to make his prophecies about my birth and that of John the Baptist, who was born to Elizabeth, wife of Zacharias.

John the Baptist's birth is recorded in the New Testament as being miraculous, as Elizabeth was supposedly "barren" and had not borne children in her old age. But, Zacharias, Elizabeth's husband, was a celibate monk who would not have sex with his wife until he eventually fathered John. Elizabeth was not old, per se—barely in her twenties—but she was older than the normal childbearing age, which in

Essene and Jewish society was quite young, around fifteen to sixteen years of age. Still, John the Baptist's birth was wrongly accredited as miraculous by the writers of the New Testament and the leaders of the early Christian church.

In the case of my mother, Mary, and my birth, it was prophesied that she would bear a child to the Holy Spirit. My mother became espoused to my father, Joseph Barsabbas. During that two-year espousal period, according to Essene tradition, the espoused couple were not supposed to have sexual intercourse. However, my parents, possibly in the throes of passion, did have sex, contrary to the rules, and I was conceived during the two-year betrothal period. My father could have put my mother away and not married her, even though he was obviously a willing participant in the sexual encounter. He refused to do that.

It is interesting to note some important things here. The priest impersonating Gabriel prophesied that Mary would be a virgin and I would be sired by the Holy Spirit. Both these prophesied conditions were true. When I was born, my mother, according to Essene tradition, was considered a virgin even though she had sexual intercourse with my father before their marriage. In Essene society, a girl remained a virgin until she married.

The second part of the prophecy—that there would be an immaculate conception through the Holy Spirit impregnating my mother—was also true, in a sense. My father, Joseph, though a humble carpenter, was an important member of Essene society, in that he had direct familial lineage with King David. For ceremonial purposes, my father was known as the Holy Spirit. However, there was nothing miraculous about my conception and birth. I was conceived in the normal way of all humans.

The Christian church promotes the idea of a miraculous immaculate conception and states that Mary remained a virgin until she died. My mother, however, had four other sons and five daughters with my father Joseph Barsabbas. The church never promotes or admits this fact, though I am sure that the church knows the truth. This immaculate conception, supposedly, adds to the church's credentials with respect to its being held as divine.

My mother was also of the familial lineage of King David, but it is the male side through which the relationship is recognised. This relationship with King David is a quandary for the Christian church, as the church promotes the fact of my familial relationship with King David, which would not have been true if I were fathered by the Holy Spirit of God. Incidentally, because of my familial lineage with King David, I was thought to be the kingly Messiah. John the Baptist was regarded as the priestly Messiah. Together, we were supposed to lead the Jewish nation out of Roman hegemony to become a world-ruling power. The Zealots, another cult of Judaism, and a very radical one, was very keen to become a world-ruling power. Silly! As Lucifer just opined, "I'm a lover, not a fighter."

With respect to the miracles I am accredited by the Christian church as having performed, I can assure you that I did not perform any miracles at all. I was accredited with raising Lazarus from the dead, changing water into wine, walking on water, and feeding five thousand followers with five loaves and two fishes. I did none of those things, in any miraculous sense.

You need to understand the Essenes and their method of describing happenings, called the *pesher,* or *pesharim,* technique. In the case of Lazarus, he committed a breach against Essene law, or doctrine, and was disfellowshipped, placed alive in a tomb for three days, and pronounced "dead." To the Essenes, he *was* dead: disfellowshipped and excluded from contact with anyone in Essene society. The *pesharim* technique must be used to understand that Lazarus didn't really die. So, when I called him forth from the tomb, he was still alive and could walk out.

With feeding of five thousand followers, according to the *pesharim* technique, the five loaves were five newly ordained Levites to the priesthood, and the two fishes were two Gentiles also newly ordained to the priesthood. The newly ordained priests fed the five thousand with the messages they preached. In similar fashion, I didn't change water into wine; nor did I walk on water. Understanding the use of the *pesharim* technique will make clear that I didn't perform miracles.

I clearly informed all the people who followed me that, to them, I spoke the truth in plain language, but to the others, non-Essenes and Gentiles, I spoke in parables and stories so that in hearing, they would not hear or understand, and in seeing, they would not see. In effect, to understand me, my followers needed to use the Essene *pesharim* technique.

With respect to my torture and supposed death on the cross, I was tortured before the Essene high priest, as well as the Roman governor, Pontius Pilate, as described in the New Testament scriptures. I was crucified as described. Because the Sabbath was at hand, after drinking poison and, in effect, committing suicide, I was speared in the side and pronounced dead. However, I was not dead, but I was very close to death. Had the Sabbath not been at hand, I'm sure I would have died. When they placed me in the tomb with the two "thieves"— Simon Magus and Judas Iscariot—they force-fed me with a mixture of myrrh and aloes. The purgative effects of that mixture made me vomit up the unassimilated poison, and I began to recover. They put me on a litter and carried me away secretly to recuperate at Mar Saba and, later, up north, at Cana in Galilee. Physically, I have never fully recovered from my ordeal, and they were good enough to have me permanently attended by two physicians to care for me. I eventually built my home in Rome beside the Tiber River, not far from where you built your home, Lucifer. As you well know, I often visited you, Lucifer, and I lived in Rome until I died, the same as any human man dies.

I can't say that I like death and dying very much, but that is the condition for all life on Planet Earth. Pity.

At no time, whilst a human man, did I ascend to heaven and sit at the right hand of the Lord God as part of some Holy Trinity. I have ascended to heaven and been with the Lord God as an Elohim, but never as a human man. The idea that I ascended into heaven is based upon the words of the crucified physician, Simon Magus, who said words to this effect: "He (Jesus [meaning me]) is healed"—implying that on his authority as a physician, I was divinely healed by God, through the agency of Simon himself. He and Helena also said, words to this effect: "He (Jesus [again meaning me]) has risen"—implying that I had risen from the dead and had been transported to the Lord God's presence in heaven.

The early Christian church, supposedly named after me—Jesus the Christ, the Anointed One—knew all of this but failed to make it clear to the Jewish and Gentile converts to Christianity. Not to tell the converts about the *pesharim* technique, and how it must be used to understand the meaning of the so-called miracles, was very wrong; but I'm sure it added to the number of converts to Christianity and the money that went into the church's coffers.

The Second Coming presumes that there was, in similar fashion, a First Coming. For me, there have been many "comings" to Planet Earth. The first one was when, as an Elohim, I was given leadership of Project Planet Earth by the Lord God. In that capacity, my friends and I subdued the planet, stocked it with vegetation, fish, birds, and animals, and, eventually, created human beings in our own image. Over the 200,000 years that followed—during the time that dominion over Planet Earth was ceded to Lucifer and his crew—I returned to Planet Earth numerous times as an Elohim, and also as a human being. Sometimes I came as a human woman, and sometimes as a human man. The last time I came to Planet Earth was to live in Palestine as the man Jesus, about two thousand years ago.

The last time I came down to Planet Earth as a human being is the time that has caused so much controversy. That was never my intent in coming. I had spoken with the Lord God about what I should do next, and he suggested that my personal development might benefit from some time in the Essene sect of Judaism. I didn't know why He suggested this course of action, but I knew a little about the Essenes and thought that my character might benefit. So, I viewed all the potential parents and chose Mary and Joseph; it didn't take much manoeuvring to make a match between them. After all, they had known each other most of their lives. Joseph had always been physically attracted to Mary, and vice versa.

I grew up as a normal boy in Palestine at that time. I learned carpentry with my father, and we attended synagogue on the Sabbath, with men and women segregated, as was Essene custom. I never lectured the congregation at twelve years old as the Egyptian god Horus supposedly did. After I left my body—which is another way of saying, after I died—the Christian ministers made that up to attract more Gentile followers, I expect.

As I was growing up, I knew and was friends with John, the son of Elizabeth and Zacharias. He later became known as John the Baptist. The relationship between us later became complicated, as you know. John and I knew that there were great expectations among the Essenes for both of us. The fact of my birth and direct relationship with King David through Joseph, my father, seemed to count a lot among the Essenes. Frankly, I couldn't see the importance or the point in being the kingly Messiah, nor could I see the importance of John being the priestly Messiah. To me, though not so much to John, it was absurd that John and I were to lead the Jewish nation into becoming a world power that would vanquish the evil Romans.

John baptised me in the River Jordan, and I was regarded as a disciple of John's for a brief period. I never agreed with the strict ascetic practices and message of the Essenes or John the Baptist. It was, as some branches of Christianity would have it today, salvation by works and not by grace. I considered then, and I still do, that it is the love we show one another, and the love we show the Lord God, that really counts, not how many hours a day we prayed and fasted. This attitude separated me from John, and I was eventually pejoratively labelled Wicked Priest and the Man of a Lie. Eventually, when people started to listen to me and follow my example, my followers—my friends, really—were labelled "seekers after smooth things."

My ministry began when I was about thirty years of age. I never wanted to have a ministry or to be followed by droves of people as though I were someone special. I have never considered myself as special, per se, but people were somehow drawn to me, and I was co-opted into talking to them. But my message wasn't John's message; it wasn't the strict Essene message.

Things changed and got worse for me when I became enlightened in regard to understanding who we all are. It was amazing to realise that we were the Elohim spoken of in the Pentateuch and elsewhere in the Bible. *Wow! We are gods!* I couldn't help myself; I had to tell everyone who would listen. Of course, I didn't know who I had been, that I was the Jesus mentioned in the Bible. There is a conscious division, or divider, between each life we live, so that we're are unaware of who we were in former lives.

The idea of past lives is not widely held in Essene of Jewish society. So, there is little or no basis for considering that we might all be Elohim in former incarnations. The enlightening moment for me came when I realised that Psalm 82:6 was speaking directly to me. It said, "Ye are gods." I couldn't disbelieve, and I had to tell people about my discovery, my message, and my gospel. This really brought down the wrath of the Essene and Jewish authorities. It was bad enough to have thrown out the money changers from the temple and to cut short their lucrative fiscal manoeuvrings, but to then tell everyone that at some time in the past we were all gods was more than the authorities could bear. If we were all gods at some time, it lowered the importance of the authorities in the people's eyes, and those in power could not bear that.

The Christian church relies quite heavily on the book of Revelation to predict my Second Coming, where I will take dominion over Planet Earth, wresting it from Lucifer—Satan, the devil, who bears the mark of the Beast: 666. We don't know who authored Revelation. The style of writing differs greatly from the elegant Greek style of John who wrote the Gospel of John. It appears that it was loosely and poorly translated from the Aramaic of John of the island of Patmos. From the text, it is not clear whether the subject matter is a prophecy about future times or times contemporary with John.

I am not implying that the end times, whenever that happens, will not be a dangerous time for all human beings. Revelation heralds worldwide war, which might indicate nuclear wars. Currently, we have a nuclear stand-off between the North Korean leader, Kim Jong-un, and the president of the United States of America, Donald Trump. Additionally, there are numerous other countries possessing nuclear weapons. Planet Earth seems to be in a unique and precarious position.

However, dominion over Planet Earth will pass easily and smoothly from the Arch-Elohim Lucifer to me, the Elohim Jesus, when the Lord God decides to cede Planet Earth, the gift he promised me nearly 200,000 years ago. It's the Lord God's decision, and I expect it could happen anytime within the next 165,000 years.

As we have both said, Lucifer and I are "Lovers, not fighters"; we have been friends and family for billions of years—that will not change. So, there will be no so-called

Second Coming. That term is a concoction of the Christian religion to keep the adherents of Christianity in line and in check; and the leadership of the churches in what they consider their rightful place of power over the "flock." That doesn't preclude the Daemon Corporation from causing trouble and fomenting nuclear war. The only losers in nuclear war will be human beings. Spirit beings—the Elohim—are not affected, as Elohim are immortal with everlasting life.

Thus, with those closing comments from Jesus, the interview with Lucifer ended.

CHAPTER 13

ADDENDUM: AN ANALYSIS
OF UNDERSTANDING ELOHIM

God is an unprovable hypothesis. I cannot prove He exists but, neither can anyone prove that He doesn't exist.

There are two levels of Elohim. The upper level is Yahweh Elohim, translated as "the Lord God"; Christianity often calls Him "Father." The lower level is Elohim, usually translated as "God" or "gods." Sometimes, the Bible does not differentiate between Yahweh Elohim and the Elohim. I expect that this is because the writers and assemblers of the various books of the Bible didn't know that they must, as exhorted in 2 Timothy 2:15, "Study to show yourself approved unto God, a workman that needeth not to be ashamed, rightly dividing the word of truth." Naturally, it is very important to understand whom one is addressing or discussing.

The Lord God—Yahweh Elohim—created all the other Elohim. The first Elohim He created was Michael, then Lucifer—the Morning Star, or the Shining One—who were archangels, or arch-Elohim. How long Yahweh Elohim and

Dr. John Sjostedt

Arch-Elohim Michael and Lucifer worked together is not known. Eventually, however, Yahweh Elohim created other archangels (arch-Elohim). He also created guardian angels (guardian Elohim), and also what might be called ordinary (or unranked) Elohim, such as the Elohim Jesus and his friends, and they worked together throughout the universe. Our universe is estimated to be about 13.8 billion years (BY) old, and our galaxy, the Milky Way, is estimated to be 13.1 BY old. Planet Earth is estimated to be 4.453 BY old, and our moon is estimated to be 4.35 BY old. By contrast, the Andromeda galaxy is estimated to be 9.006 BY old.

It is possible that Jesus and his co-workers were created at the very commencement of our universe. However, we do not have any way of knowing when Yahweh Elohim created the Elohim. It is estimated that Yahweh Elohim initially created some 240,000 Elohim who, as of today, would be 13.1 BY old. But, in my humble opinion, it is more likely that the Elohim Jesus and his fellow Elohim co-workers were created sometime between the creation of Planet Earth (4.453 BY ago) and the appearance of the dinosaurs (sometime between 231 and 243 million years ago). The Elohim Jesus and his fellow Elohim had to have been created before humankind (the species *Homo sapiens*), whose appearance on Planet Earth is estimated to have been some 200,000 years ago.

I would propose that Yahweh Elohim, the Lord God, is the ultimate Creator of our universe and all things in it—except, perhaps, the humans, the men and women, that the Elohim Jesus and his co-workers created when tasked to create and re-create Planet Earth. However, the creation and re-creation of Planet Earth was done under the auspices of Yahweh Elohim; ultimately, He was in charge and responsible for everything.

How many humans were created by the Elohim Jesus and his friends? We do not know. However, it is estimated that each Elohim initially created four humans, with an equal number of men and women (that is, two males and two females). It is estimated that there were approximately one million humans on Planet Earth when the Archangel Lucifer was given dominion over the earth. We see great diversity among the humans on Planet Earth. This probably means that there is diversity among the Elohim, if humans were created in their own image. This suggests that Yahweh Elohim loves and wants diversity.

━━━◦◦◦◦◦━━━

The population of Planet Earth is now, as of this writing, estimated to be about 7,632,819,325 billion[25]. Indications are that this level of population is unsustainable.

It seems to be generally accepted by most religions and churches that Yahweh Elohim—or, the Father, as they mostly call Him—provides guardian angels (guardian Elohim) for most/many/all people, groups, kingdoms, countries, and governments to help and protect them. If this is true and correct, then there may be well more than 7.6 billion guardian Elohim, or angels, with us on Planet Earth today.

Whilst all living children born into the world have a human life force, do they also each have an Elohim residing with them or somehow accompanying them until death, in

---

[25] Wikipedia: *www.worldometers.info/world-population/*

addition to the guardian Elohim assigned to them? If the answer is yes, then there would be a total of some 15.2 billion Elohim in existence today accompanying all humans on Planet Earth. That number would not include the guardian Elohim and the Elohim who accompanied each human in years gone by and generations past. Those Elohim may now reside in the heavenly realm with the Lord God, awaiting their return to Planet Earth, if that is their choice and their free will. The potential numbers start to boggle the mind. But the task of creating an Elohim, in the face of creating a universe, does not seem too onerous for One such as Yahweh Elohim to achieve. We can imagine that 20 to 30 billion Elohim would barely be sufficient to adequately staff the billions of galaxies in our One's universe. So, it seems logical that there is much more happening on Planet Earth than merely creating humans. So, what is Yahweh Elohim's master plan? I do not yet see or understand what it is.

I am sure, though, that you can see the potential for conflict and discord among the Elohim, just as you can see the poisoned fruits of the abuse of free will in all human societies today. Consider, for example, that there is a hierarchy of galaxies, and on each galaxy, there is a hierarchy of Elohim running and governing each galaxy and populating each solar system and each suitable planet with animals, birds, marine life, and, of course, human life. The potential for competition and rivalry among the Elohim would probably be no different than it is among countries populated by humans, with human governments, churches, and businesses, just as we have here on Planet Earth. That is why Yahweh Elohim is so focused on the issue of the sullied fruits of free will among Elohim and humans, which manifest as ego in all its many forms.

It is understood that when a person dies "…the spirit returns to the God that gave it." Is that "spirit," the human life force, or the energy or imprint of human nature, or the Elohim who accompanied that human during his or her life? It seems certain that the Elohim can be pure, immortal spirit, or they can take on physical human form, as required; otherwise, the "third of the heavenly host" that followed the Arch-Elohim Lucifer to earth would not have been able to have sex with the humans on Planet Earth.

It is said, or proposed, that spirit, an Elohim, cannot easily change without the catalyst of human life and experience. So, it is possible that when humans die, and "…the spirit returns to the God that gave it," the Elohim and guardian Elohim who accompanied the human when alive, apparently return to Yahweh Elohim, waiting to accompany another human on his or her journey through life.

The roles of the Elohim may, perhaps, reverse with each human life they experience. For example, Jesus, in the interview with Lucifer, Lisa, and John, mentioned that he had come to Planet Earth many times as a human being to experience the change to his spirit that can occur through living a human life. Jesus's final time on Planet Earth as a human was the time two thousand years ago, when he was an Essene and became the source and inspiration for the Christian religion. He reports that he had been to Planet Earth many times since that tempestuous time, but as a spirit. I expect that he has played the role of guardian Elohim to numerous humans in the subsequent two thousand years.

If it is true that Yahweh Elohim's gift of free will allows each Elohim to develop in any way it chooses, then some Elohim may have very few faults or character defects, whilst others may have very many faults. Arch-Elohim Lucifer became hurt and upset—had a "tantrum," in his words—and questioned Yahweh Elohim's plan to give the Elohim Jesus Planet Earth as a gift. But, later, in the recent interview mentioned above, Arch-Elohim Lucifer indicated that he repented of his ego-prompted outburst, prostrated himself before Yahweh Elohim in humble supplication, and was forgiven.

But what of the guardian Elohim and the Elohim accompanying Hitler or Himmler or Stalin, or Mao, or Genghis Khan, or any one of probably millions of bloodthirsty brutes who have inhabited this beautiful Planet Earth throughout human history? If they, the Elohim themselves, destroy or kill, they will forfeit their eternal life. But, more than likely, they will return to Planet Earth as humans many, many, many times to experience and reexperience the wheel of life: to be born, to live their lives, and to die, over and over, until the brute within them is gone, and they have learned to love and respect life; in essence, until they have learned the lessons of free will that they needed to learn.

Through the wheel of birth, life, and death, the usually unchangeable spirit, or essence, of the Elohim learns. Eventually, all character flaws allowed by the gift of free will are eliminated, and they are perfected.

In my, unfinished fantasy book *Gabriel and Thor the Dog of War: World War I,* which is about witches and wizards, the central character, Gabriel, finds himself incapacitated in a smelly shell-hole, accompanied by a dead horse he calls Dobbin, whose severed head grins at him on one side and whose bottom points at him on the other side. I won't say more now about how and why he arrived in a shell-hole. Whilst in that shell-hole, Gabriel experiences a vision of a heavenly realm. Yahweh Elohim is there, as are everyone Gabriel knew on earth. He recognises his mother and father, his twin sister, the Archangel Michael, and others. In that heavenly realm, they look the same as they did down on earth, and because I started writing that book first, it got me stuck in a rut with respect to the Elohim.

As I started writing this book, I mistakenly began to see the Elohim's physical appearance as being the same throughout each incarnation. Let me explain this further by describing my Elohim. You will remember that I call my resident (or accompanying) Elohim, John; and my guardian Elohim, I call Lisa. Lisa is there to help me and keep me safe, and I can tell you some amazing ways she has kept me safe throughout my life. The Elohim John experiences my life and the mind-dulling miseries I have inflicted upon myself, and in my mind, he looked like me all the time. Experiencing my stupidities helped to change the spirit of the Elohim residing within or beside me. Now I realise that what I look like in this context is not particularly important; nevertheless, it got me stuck as I wrote. I don't know how many past lives I have experienced. But, an Arapaho squaw would not physically look the same as a Sioux brave, or as a French dandy or an itinerant American preacher. Yet, I got stuck there with appearances. Regardless, my accompanying/resident Elohim, John, gained experience, and that experience changed or modified the spirit within me—the John in me, so to speak—as a result of the lives I have experienced.

It might be the same spirit, or Elohim, that has inhabited

successive bodies, sometimes male, sometimes female, sometimes black African, sometimes Chinese, sometimes Japanese, sometimes European, sometimes American Indian, sometimes Indian, sometimes white American, and in this current lifetime, white European (Irish/Swedish/German) Australian. The many different bodies the Elohim spirit resided in and experienced would help to mediate and moderate the various fundamental character flaws, caused by free will, affecting the spirit of the Elohim I currently identify as John.

Here I go again. This whole Elohim business is a complex thing, and there are numerous different permutations. What if, in my case, there is no Elohim John? What if there is only the guardian Elohim I call Lisa? She alone is with me from my birth until my death. She protects me, as a guardian angel, and she may accompany me and experience everything I experience throughout my life, and, thus, the experiences to which she is exposed change, or modify and moderate, the spirit within her.

I mentioned above brutish humans like Hitler, Himmler, Stalin, and Mao, to name just a few. How does an Elohim respond when assigned to live in or accompany such brutes, and many others? I cannot imagine that an Elohim could come out of such encounters unscathed. The spirit of the Elohim must be terribly affected and horribly influenced.

If there is a God. ...

I got "dumped on" last year (on December 13, 2017) by one of my patients, Sally, whom I regard as a friend. I regard most of my patients as friends, but I am very close to her in particular. She is the incest victim I described earlier, who, when she was a twelve-year-old girl, witnessed her father murdering her dog. She then attacked her father with the shovel he gave her to bury the dog's corpse, after which she ran away to work on the streets of Sydney. She eventually went to TAFE (Tertiary and Further Education) and learned her trade as a chef. She is a very good chef and has cooked for royalty. She gave me a huge chunk of fruit cake for Christmas (which I consumed in the weeks that followed—so much for my diet ... but it was Christmastime, after all). But she made a mistake with this fruit cake; she forgotten to put the two-dollar gold coins in it. There was not even one gold coin anywhere. (I sent her an SMS to notify her of her error.)

Back to the point of her dumping on me. On the above-mentioned Wednesday, she did her normal thing of beating around the bush for three-quarters of our counselling session, trying to avoid talking to me about the issues that were troubling her. I don't recall if I told you that her partner of seventeen years died about two years ago, and she can't get past her grief. Also, her little fifteen-year-old Jack Russell terrier, Spooky, bit her three times that week. Sally has been suicidal in the recent past, and I felt sick when she said, "When Spooky dies, there will be nothing left for me to live for! I'll let you know when I'm going to do it." (By the way, Spooky died towards the end of February 2018.)

Anyway, she dumped her hurt and grief upon me, as many of my patients do, but Sally was vociferous. This was very confrontational for me, whilst writing this book, as she took God/gods to task for all the evils in the world.

She said things like, "If there is a God/gods, why does/ do He/they allow all the pain and suffering in the world?";

"If there is a God/gods, why does He/they allow all the evil people in the world to thrive and prosper?"; "I don't think there is a God/gods—we are here on earth alone, trying to battle things out on our own"; "Earth is our hell." She actually said much more as well, and used some choice language to emphasise her pain and suffering.

Whilst listening to her, I could recall times when I said similar things about the existence of God/gods. I recalled that once, in the backyard of my now-deceased mate Merv Bell's house in Cardiff, a suburb of Newcastle, I shook my fist at the heavens and called God/gods a "capricious prick." I had no work at the time, except driving taxis in Newcastle, which I hated, and I had just been thrown out of (disfellowshipped, made *dead*, like Lazarus) a so-called Christian church: the Worldwide Church of God (WCG), of which I had chosen to be a member. So, the date when I berated God/gods must have been immediately before September 1, 1980. The minister of the church, as he disfellowshipped me, said, "You shall be cast into everlasting darkness where is weeping and gnashing of teeth." *Nice of him to be so kind,* I thought at the time.

I can now picture God, sitting on His throne, looking down at this poor benighted fool shaking his fists at the heavens and berating God for his own mistakes and failings. My moment of berating God has proved useful in some of counselling sessions with patients, though, often serving as an example of my lunacy. When appropriate, I will say to patients, "Why don't you get up off your arse and do something useful with your life?" It took me until 1993, at forty-nine years of age, to get up off my arse, start at university, and "do something with my life." I must be a slow learner, but after nearly ten years at the University of Newcastle, NSW,

Australia, I graduated with my doctoral research and higher degree in psychology. So, now I'm a doctor—I always wanted to be a doctor.

Nevertheless, in all that time, I never really doubted that there was/is a God/gods, though I remain an agnostic. I'm using the term *God/gods,* as I've done throughout this book, to denote Yahweh Elohim (or Lord God), and gods or Elohim, though I did not know until relatively recently that the Lord God had first created the Elohim, and then Elohim created humans (*Homo sapiens*), as discussed in earlier chapters.

I suspect that Yahweh Elohim's plan has played out as it has because He has not become directly involved in the affairs of humankind, preferring to allow us to sort out our affairs ourselves. And, we have not done a very good job of sorting, what with the raving lunatic Kim Jong-un and the mad hatter in the White House threatening to wipe out our world in a nuclear holocaust. It's all ego and pride.

If Yahweh Elohim wanted to show us a better way, allowing us to live through this madness created by humans, then He will undoubtedly prepare us for that better way as no other situation ever could. But does this earthly mess created by humans absolve Yahweh Elohim and His Elohim of complicity in this earthly farce?

The easy answer for me is to say, "No, Yahweh Elohim is not responsible for this mess. It's our mess; we created it." But, instead, I think we must view this situation much more closely.

Of course, Yahweh Elohim could step in and bring this situation to a close in a millisecond. But, if He were to do that, would all of us learn? Would we all appreciate the pivotal role that ego, pride, and greed have played in this present lunacy?

Those ambitious individuals eager for money, power, and prestige are, it seems to me, the ones who have delivered us into this potentially dangerous chapter in the evolution of our peoples and our planet. They are our so-called leaders, our politicians, and our priests. I think we are all aware that there are a few among us—we may not know them all—who have sufficient power and wealth to allow their egos to foment wars for personal profit and gain, to pollute our beautiful planet, to denude our forests and thoughtlessly ruin the habitats of poor farmers, animals, and birds. I don't think many of them would have learned.

In saying that I do not wish to imply that we are all filled with the sins of the ego or expressions of the ego. No, I do not consider that most humans are filled with ego. I consider that most ordinary people try to be good and caring, and mostly succeed in that endeavour, and are not out-of-control egotists. Their lives centre on the mundane tasks of working so that they can care for and provide for their families. They aren't perfect (yet), but they are not egomaniacs like some.

What are the sins—forgive me for using a churchy term—and expressions of the ego? Some of the sins are narcissism, a sense of entitlement (earned or unearned), greed, pride, aggression, anger, self-centredness and concern only for the self, and many more.

Osho, in his book *Turn On, Tune In and Drop the Lot*, says:

> The enemy is the ego, and unless the ego disappears life remains a hell. The ego creates darkness, the ego creates blindness. The ego becomes a rock and it does not allow your life to flow. The ego creates a separation

from existence and the separation creates all
kinds of miseries.

The churches would have us believe that the return of Jesus and the setting up of his rule on earth would bring an end to the current lunacy we see playing out before us. But, whilst Yahweh Elohim can (but does not) take human lives, the Elohim, including the returned Jesus, cannot do so. In the chaos following Jesus's return, many human lives may be lost, and the Elohim might, inadvertently, be involved. So, the so-called return of Jesus the Christ will not be the panacea that all the Christian religions are hoping for.

I trust that a nuclear holocaust is not inevitable; I'll be a goner like everyone else. But, the book of Revelation seems to imply that such a situation may occur. This will mean that many billions of humans will die, as will many land animals and birds. At the end of it all, the human and animal populations on Planet Earth will be completely decimated, and only a very small fraction of the 7.6 billion humans currently on earth will remain alive. Of course, the Elohim remaining on Planet Earth, being pure spirit, will be unaffected by the conflagration; but, as far as humans are concerned, only a few will survive, in small groups dotted about the earth.

Yahweh Elohim's plan for Planet Earth will have been successful, though, despite the suffering of all life involved. This sounds completely heartless, and my friend Sally would totally condemn what I have said and suggested. Nevertheless, in the chaos of a man-made calamity, such as a nuclear holocaust, much of the evil on this earth will be destroyed, and whatever evil beings remain will clearly see the fruits of their perfidiousness. Of course, we all know that the evil people will have their hidey-holes or bolt-holes or jetliners to ride out the calamity. But what of the rest of us?

Some sects of Christianity—the Baptists and other similar denominations—will have a promise of the *rapture* (we used to call it the "rupture" in the WCG), where the "elect of God" will be transported to heaven to ride out the storm before the return of Christ to earth. I wonder, will humans be provided with bottles of oxygen? I say that because there is no atmosphere up there.

Similarly, the obedient, faithful, and righteous members of the WCG, into which I was supposedly called to be one of the "chosen and elect," would flee in jetliners to a "place of safety" sometime in 1975. The so-called place of safety for members of the WCG was supposedly the ancient city of Petra in the Muslim country of Jordan. The year 1975 came and went, and none of us fled to the safety of Petra. The church announced that the flight to a place of safety, where the righteous in Christ would be saved from the Armageddon to come, was correct; they only got the date wrong.

Yahweh Elohim created the Elohim and gave us free will and limitless possibilities. The Elohim (a small group of them), some 200,000 years ago, created *Homo sapiens*, males and females, in their own image and gave humankind free will. Without free will, the Elohim and humankind would be automatons, robots with limited possibilities. Free will is wonderful, but, as you are no doubt are aware by now, free will can lead to a multitude of thorny problems, not the least of which is rampant, uncontrolled ego. But this is why the Lord God, if He exists, has not stepped in and taken overall control of Planet Earth—just yet.

CONCLUSION

Every human child has human life force within him or her throughout the lifetime. As the child grows into an adult and, finally, into old age (or sickness prematurely), the life force begins to dwindle and wane until, ultimately, the human dies. Where that life force goes is unknown. Energy can be converted in form, but, according to science, it can neither be created nor destroyed.

Is human life force the same as the spirit within and, perhaps, alongside a human being? The answer is no. Spirit is a being, an entity, that accompanies and resides within every human being on Planet Earth. Spirit, therefore, is more than human life force or energy transmuted into some other form. The spirit of which I speak is the Spirit of Yahweh Elohim, the Lord God of this universe, who endows every child, every human, with a portion of His infinite being. Throughout this book, I have called the form that this spirit takes Elohim, or God/gods.

When the human being dies, the human life force leaves the body and is, perhaps, converted into universal energy. The spirit then "... returns to the God that gave it." That spirit, that Elohim, endowed with free will as it is, awaits its return to Planet Earth to reexperience life in another human body and lifetime. Thus, the spirit within will be changed in the only way that an Elohim can be changed: by living and experiencing human life. The aim of this act repeated over and over, is to modify and moderate the free will of that Elohim until all vestiges of ego are eliminated. The spirit is not a robot or an automaton, but its free will allows it to be a pure spirit. The spirit then attains nirvana and anatta—no self, no soul, no being.

EPILOGUE

After I resigned from the Australian Regular Army Intelligence Corps in 1970 (I had been an army spook for a short time and a Vietnamese linguist), I went to a fundamentalist Bible college in Pasadena, California, in 1976–77, hoping to become a minister of the church I foolishly joined.

The so-called Christian church and personality cult I joined followed most of the Jewish customs, such as keeping the Saturday Sabbath, observing the Jewish Holy Days, distinguishing between clean and unclean foods, and, of course, tithing. (This is the WCG described earlier.) In 1976, I attended the Feast of Tabernacles, in Port Dickson, Malaysia, and then took the worst flight I have ever experienced, courtesy of Alitalia, out of Singapore.

After Malaysia and Singapore, my first stop on my way to England and the United States was Israel. We landed at Tel Aviv's Lod airport, and I took a *sherut* (an elongated yellow Mercedes-Benz car), which held a lot of packed-in travellers, to Jerusalem. I felt a strange excitement as we drew up to the YMCA opposite the King David Hotel near the old city of Jerusalem, located less than a kilometre away, as I recall.

Strangely, I felt like I had come home.

I had never felt that way before, even in Australia and Adamstown, where I was born.

I spent over three months in Jerusalem, walking about

the old city, visiting the wailing wall, and working on the Jerusalem dig (where I briefly met Dr Benjamin Mazar, the archaeologist. I visited the garden tomb near the Arab bus depot outside the Damascus Gate of the old city, where Jesus was supposedly entombed after his crucifixion. (This is, of course, untrue, as Jesus was crucified at Golgotha, Qumran, and was entombed below Golgotha. But I didn't know that then.)

Not only did I have the strangest feeling that I had returned home when I arrived in Jerusalem, but I also had the strange impression that I was one of the Roman soldiers, perhaps a centurion, at the crucifixion of Jesus in Golgotha, Qumran. Perhaps I was the Roman soldier who speared Jesus in the side and watched the blood and water flow from the wound. Perhaps I was the one who proclaimed that Jesus was dead, firmly believing he *was* dead. I also had the strangest feeling that I, as that soldier, repented of my sins against Jesus and became a Christian, a follower of Jesus.

In my many lives, I have very often been a soldier or a priest. In this life, I was a soldier, and then I went to Bible college to train to become a minister of a fundamentalist church. Fortunately, I did not become a minister. I was made "dead" to that church when they disfellowshipped me and "… cast me into everlasting darkness where there shall be weeping and gnashing of teeth," just like the Essenes disfellowshipped Lazarus. (I'm not saying I was Lazarus, by the way.)

Before the lifetime with Jesus at the crucifixion, I had other lifetimes on earth. I was a farmer in Mesopotamia (modern-day Iraq), along the Euphrates River, when I was conscripted into the Babylonian army, eventually rising to the rank of general. I was a squaw with two children at an army fort in the United States. I was an Indian brave, probably a medicine man; an Indian Sadhu at Varanasi, on the Ganges; and an itinerant Christian preacher trudging the back roads of the United States, preaching the so-called Christian message of Jesus the Christ and his imminent return.

I expect that each time I visited Planet Earth to live as a human, I learned something new that helped moderate and modify my spirit—my accompanying Elohim—and each time my human body died my "… spirit returned to the God that gave it," the Lord God, our One. I don't know how many times I have come to Planet Earth to experience human life. But each human lifetime eventually ended, and each human body ultimately died, and that must have been heartbreaking for me to experience over and over and over, again and again and again.

Buddha was once quoted as saying he remembered once being a dolphin. According to Buddha, when enlightenment finally comes, we enter nirvana—nothingness. The problem with that is, I like it here, and I really don't want to leave. But I'm sick and tired of dying. There's got to be a better way. I did talk about this earlier, if you recall. It's like they say: "Life sucks, and then you die!" Sorry for being negative.

Let me just add this: Despite academic controversy concerning the discipline of palaeontology, with the dating of ancient manuscripts, we know that the god Jesus, the Elohim Jesus, lived as a human being on earth, because the evidence of his life, and that of John the Baptist and the celibate monks of the Essene religion in Qumran, is recorded in the Dead Sea Scrolls.

The Elohim Jesus, who initially created and re-created the Planet Earth under the auspices of Yahweh Elohim, the

Lord God, was back on earth about two thousand years ago as a human being. He was recognised and accepted by a sect of the Jews, the Essenes, into which he was born and raised and to which he belonged. He was recognised and accepted by members of the Essenes as their kingly Messiah; John the Baptist was the priestly Messiah.

Printed in the United States
By Bookmasters